AA

Pocket Book of Britain's
WALKS

D1317052

Produced by AA Publishing
© AA Media Limited 2010
Reprinted March and May 2011

Published by AA Publishing (a trading name of AA Media Limited, whose registered office is
Fanum House, Basing View, Basingstoke, Hampshire RG21 4EA; registered number 06112600).

Enabled by [OS Ordnance Survey] This product includes mapping data licensed from the Ordnance Survey® with
the permission of the Controller of Her Majesty's Stationery Office. © Crown
Copyright 2011. All rights reserved. Licence number 100021153.

ISBNs: 978-0-7495-6640-1 and 978-0-7495-6627-2 (SS)

A CIP catalogue record for this book is available from the British Library.

The contents of this book are believed correct at the time of printing. Nevertheless, the publishers
cannot be held responsible for any errors or omissions or for changes in the details given in this
book or for the consequences of any reliance on the information it provides. This does not affect
your statutory rights. We have tried to ensure accuracy in this book, but things do change and we
would be grateful if readers would advise us of any inaccuracies they may encounter.

We have taken all reasonable steps to ensure that these walks are safe and achievable by walkers
with a realistic level of fitness. However, all outdoor activities involve a degree of risk and the
publishers accept no responsibility for any injuries caused to readers whilst following these walks.
For more advice on using this book and walking safely see page 8.

Visit AA Publishing at theAA.com/shop

Cartography provided by the Mapping Services Department of AA Publishing

Repro and colour separation by Keene Repro

Printed and bound by Leo Paper Products, China

A04743

AA

Pocket Book of Britain's
WALKS

Contents

CENTRAL ENGLAND

NORTHERN ENGLAND

WALES

SCOTLAND

Introduction

by Roly Smith,
President of the Outdoor Writers' and Photographers' Guild

There can be no doubt that Britain is a nation of walkers. It is now the most popular outdoor leisure activity by a long way, with more than three quarters of the adult population (77 per cent, or about 38 million people) walking for pleasure at least once a month. That's many more than go angling, play golf or watch football, activities traditionally the most popular of outdoor pursuits.

To be more accurate, we are a nation of ramblers, and the use of that gentler, very British term is significant. In America, walkers are known as hikers or backpackers, and in continental Europe they are excursionists, all signifying a much more serious enterprise. Rambling, on the other hand, means to wander where you fancy or to generally rove about. This book is aimed at those ramblers who want to find out more, to seek out the relatively undiscovered corners, and delve behind the usual tourist board clichés.

By far the best way to see and really experience the fascinating landscapes which make up the British Isles is on foot. Car or coach-bound tourists can only expect to receive a packaged and sanitised view of Britain as seen through a window. It is only the walker who is really able explore the warp and weft of the land, to seek out its real character, and to experience the indefinable sense of history which lies deeply ingrained in every field, hedge, hill and dale.

Why Walk?

Apart from the physical pleasure of 'getting away from it all', there are many other reasons why walking is best. In these increasingly health-conscious days, walking is now recognised as the nearest thing you can get to perfect exercise. You can go as fast or as slow as you like, you are exercising just about every muscle, and you are getting plenty of fresh air. And perhaps most importantly, it is free. There's no need to go to the gym if there's a footpath outside your door.

The government's Chief Medical Officer, recently recommended that adults should take at least 30 minutes of moderate physical exercise, such as walking, five days a week. It is recognised that regular, brisk walking will improve the performance of your heart, lungs and circulation, lower your blood pressure and reduce the risk of heart disease and strokes.

It can also help manage your weight, reduce the risk of diabetes and colon, breast and lung cancer, and improve flexibility and strength in joints, muscles and bones, thus reducing the risk of osteoporosis. There are mental benefits too, as it has been shown that walking can also improve your mood and reduce the harmful effects of stress.

Where to Walk

Apart from its health-giving qualities, another important factor in walking in

Britain is the wonderfully varied and outstandingly beautiful scenery with which our islands are blessed. There are few other countries in the world where, during the course of a day's walk, you can pass from airy coastal cliffs or sandy beaches, through lovely riverside meadows and woods to crag-bound lakes and towering mountains.

Humans have shaped the British landscape over 10,000 years of history, and it has accurately been described as a palimpsest – a living manuscript that has been written on over and over again. With a little help, such as that given by the expert authors within this volume, it can also be read like a book.

There are many walks to spectacular natural landscapes, from the views of the wild Torridon Hills from Loch Kernsary near Poolewe in the Scottish Highlands to the heathery staircase of the Roman Steps

from Cwm Bychan in the rugged Rhiniog Mountains of Snowdonia. In between are the peaty wildernesses of Kinder Scout in the Dark Peak and the isolated moorland summit of High Willhays, the highest point of Dartmoor.

Britain is a land rich in history and folklore. You can re-trace the steps of the legendary outlaw Robin Hood through the ancient woodlands of Sherwood Forest, or see where the Devil himself was reputed to have dug his eponymous Dyke on the rolling South Downs to let in the sea and flood local churches.

Old Nick is also said to be responsible for the deep depression known as The Devil's Beef Tub, near Moffat in the Southern Uplands of Scotland, a place where the reiving clans hid their rustled cattle. The Merry Maidens stone circle on the Penwith peninsula in Cornwall is claimed to be a group of young girls

Below Cook Monument, North York Moors National Park

Above: The beautiful beach at Bude

caught dancing on the Sabbath and turned them to stone – a common fate commemorated in many of our prehistoric stone circles.

Other walks dip into the rich treasury of British history, such as the impressive ruins of Middleham Castle in Yorkshire, the favoured home of the future Richard III; the mountain-rimmed scene of the infamous Glencoe Massacre in Scotland, and the elegant cathedral spire and close at Salisbury in Wiltshire.

Many of the areas visited are renowned for their wildlife, such as the butterfly-haunted reed beds of Wicken Fen in Norfolk, and the wildfowl haven of the Martin Mere Wetland Centre in Lancashire. Other paths follow in the footsteps of the great writers, painters or poets who have been inspired by the ever-changing scenery and timeless sense of history.

Walkers' Rights

There are 140,000 miles (225,000km) of public rights of way in England and Wales, and following the passing of the Countryside and Rights of Way (CROW) Act in 2000, there is also now the right of free access to 6,250 square miles (16,200sq km) of open country, mainly mountains and moorlands. In Scotland, there is a de facto right of access above the enclosed foothills. The government has recently announced that it intends to introduce the same 'right to roam' along the 2,733 miles (4,400km) of the English and Welsh coastline, under the Coastal Access and

Marine Act which received royal assent in November 2009.

Elsewhere, you should keep to those rights of way which have the same status in law as a highway like the M1 motorway. Therefore, if you find one that is blocked, you have the right to clear it to allow your free passage. However, we do not recommend you argue or try to force a way; it is better to report the blockage to the relevant local authority footpath officer. If you stray from a right of way, unless you are on access land, technically you will be trespassing, but unless you do damage you cannot be prosecuted, despite what some signs still say. All the routes in this book have been rigorously checked and are either on rights of way or on well-established, legal paths.

When out in the country, you should always respect the life of the people who live and work there, especially the farmers, who have to such a large extent created the landscapes we know and love today. The Countryside Code is a common sense set of principles which is probably best encapsulated by the maxim: 'Take only photographs, leave only footprints'.

Happy walking!

Using this Book

The *Pocket Book of Britain's Walks* divides the country into six regional sections with up to 18 walks per section.

The route of each walk is shown on a map, and clear directions help you follow the walk. The step-by-step directions also mention notable places to see along the way.

Route Information

A panel with each walk details the total distance, terrain, conditions underfoot, parking, public toilets and any special conditions that apply, such as restricted access or level of dog friendliness. The minimum time suggested for the walk is for reasonably fit walkers and doesn't allow for stops. An indication of the gradients you will encounter is shown by the rating ▲▲▲ (no steep slopes) to ▲▲▲ (several very steep slopes). Walks are also rated for their difficulty – those rated ●●● are usually shorter and easier with little total ascent. The hardest walks are marked ●●●.

Parking and Getting Started

Many of the car parks suggested are public, but occasionally you may find you have to park on the roadside or in a lay-by. Please be considerate when you leave your car, ensuring that access roads or gates are not blocked and that other vehicles can pass safely. The start of each walk is given as a six-figure grid reference prefixed by two letters indicating the 100-km square of the National Grid to which it refers. Each walk has a suggested Ordnance Survey Explorer map where you'll find more information on using grid references.

Dog Friendliness

Keep your dog under control at all times, especially around livestock, and obey local byelaws and other dog control notices. Remember, it is against the law to let your dog foul in many public areas, especially in villages and towns.

The route information often contains specific advice regarding the dog friendliness of the walk. Not all routes in this book are appropriate for dog walkers so do read the advice provided before setting out.

Walking in Safety

All these walks are suitable for any reasonably fit person, but less experienced walkers should try the easier walks first. Although each walk here has been researched with a view to minimising the risks to the walkers who follow its route, no walk in the countryside can be considered to be completely free from risk. Walking will always require a degree of common sense and judgement to ensure that it is as safe as possible.

❑ Be particularly careful on cliff paths and in upland terrain, where the consequences of a slip can be very serious.

❑ Remember always to check tidal conditions before walking along the seashore.

❑ Some sections of route are by, or cross, busy roads. Take care and remember traffic is a danger even on minor country lanes.

Above: The view towards High Willhays, shrouded in mist

❏ Be careful around farmyard machinery and livestock, especially if you have children with you.

❏ Be aware of the consequences of changes in the weather and check the forecast before you set out. Carry spare clothing and a torch if you are walking in the winter months. Remember that the weather can change very quickly at any time of the year, and in moorland and heathland areas, mist and fog can make route finding much harder. Don't set out in these conditions unless you are confident of your navigation skills in poor visibility. In summer, remember to take account of the heat and sun; wear a hat and sunscreen, and always remember to carry spare water with you.

❏ On walks away from centres of population, you should carry a whistle and survival bag. If you do have an accident requiring the emergency services, make a note of your position as accurately as possible and dial 999.

Southwest England

The Southwest of England stretches from the rural heart of England to the cliffs and coves of the Lizard and Land's End.

Tiny fishing villages and smugglers' haunts contrast with bustling seaside resorts such as Newquay and Penzance, and the rolling farmland of central Devon. Despite the extensive granite uplands rising inland, you're never far from the sea, with Atlantic breakers crashing against the north coast and the gentler waters of the English Channel washing the south coast.

The Southwest boasts two national parks: the wild and extensive upland bogs of Dartmoor – with the giant granite blocks or tors such as High Wilhays (see Walk 7) – and the cliffs and rolling heaths of Exmoor. Areas of Outstanding Natural Beauty encompass large stretches of the Cornish coast, Bodmin Moor and parts of Devon and Dorset, as well as the Quantock Hills and North Wessex Downs. There are lengths of designated Heritage Coast, with dramatic landscape and rich history, Sites of Special Scientific Interest such as the Teign Valley woodlands in Devon (see Walk 4) and a wealth of natural history to explore in the uncultivated land of the Cotswold escarpment, or the rugged, recessed gorges of the Mendips.

The Southwest is an area rich in legend and ancient history. The hills of the Dorset and the Wessex Downs are scored by ancient earthworks and decorated with chalk figures, including the celebrated and enigmatic Cerne Abbas Giant (see Walk 3). In the rolling downs of Devon and Dorset there are echoes of Alfred's Kingdom of Wessex in the late 9th century, although the latter is now a name more commonly associated with the poet and novelist Thomas Hardy (see Walk 1).

There is no shortage of footpaths and trackways to explore. Inland walks now quiet places that once had wider fame – such as the ancient Devon town of Bampton (see Walk 6), once known as a setting for wool and cattle markets and featuring an 11th-century church. In Bridford, on the edge of Dartmoor (see Walk 4), the 15th-century church stands on the site of a 12th-century chapel, and contains a magnificent carved rood screen dating from 1508.

If you are looking for spectacular scenery, then the beautiful clifftop grasslands at Bude (see Walk 10) and tumbling sea cliffs at Portreath (see Walk 11), both on Cornwall's Atlantic coast, are for you. At the opposite end of the scale, attractive historic towns offer a rich urban landscape to discover. In Salisbury, for example (see Walk 15), attractions include the 13th-century Bishop's Palace and a series of elegant period buildings in Cathedral Close, as well as the cathedral with the tallest spire in England.

The area is rich in historic country houses set in beautiful estates. These include the exquisite Elizabethan mansion of Longleat (see Walk 16) and, in Cornwall the 16th-century Mount Edgcumbe House which stands at the heart of a beautiful 865-acre (350ha) landscaped park (Walk 9). In Wiltshire, the Palladian mansion of Lydiard House (see Walk 17) is likewise situated in beautiful parkland with an 18th-century walled garden.

Left: The spire of Salisbury Cathedral

1 By Hardy's Cottage and 'Egdon Heath'

Explore the countryside that Thomas Hardy loved – and immortalised in his celebrated novels

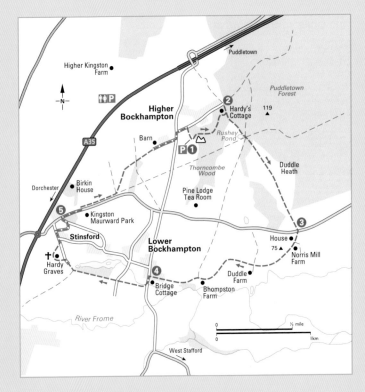

Distance 5 miles (8km)

Minimum Time 2hrs

Ascent/Gradient 328ft (100m) ▲▲▲

Level of Difficulty ●●●

Paths Woodland and heathland tracks, muddy field paths and bridleways, firm paths, road, 13 stiles

Landscape Woodland, tree-clad heath, open meadows, waterway, rolling farmland

Suggested Map OS Explorer 117 Cerne Abbas & Bere Regis or OL15 Purbeck & South Dorset

Start/Finish Grid reference: SY 725921

Dog Friendliness Not allowed in Hardy's garden or cottage; deer shooting year-round in woods – keep dogs close

Parking Thorncombe Wood (donations) below Hardy's Cottage

Public Toilets None en route; nearest north-west on A35

1 Take the steep woodland path to the right of the display boards, signposted 'Hardy's Cottage'. Turn left at the fingerpost and follow the winding route down to a crossroads of tracks, marked by a monument. Turn left for Hardy's Cottage.

2 Retrace your route up behind the cottage and bear left, signed 'Rushy Pond' on a path that bears right. At a crossroads by the pond take the path ahead signed 'Norris Mill'. Immediately fork right; the path heads down between fences, soon passing through heathland then between rhododendrons. Cross a stile and bear right. Enter a field by a stile and turn left up the field, towards a house.

3 Cross the road on to a farm track which keeps to the right of some barns. Where the track ends, bear right over a field. Cross a pair of stiles in the hedge, then go straight ahead across the fields and a drive, passing Duddle Farm (left). Cross a bridge and stile down into a field. Go straight on and bear left, following the track round the hill. Cross a stile by a converted barn and walk up the drive. At the fingerpost keep straight on through a gate. Bear left to a stile and walk along the field-edge to a gate, then walk down the field to a gate at the far corner. Go through and straight on, with the river away to your left. Go through the farmyard and along a road.

4 Turn left by Bridge Cottage. Cross the river and immediately turn right, on to a causeway. After 0.5 mile (800m) turn right, signed 'Stinsford'. Walk up and turn left into the churchyard, just below the church. Pass the church to your left, and the Hardy graves to your right. Leave by the top gate and walk up the road. Pass Casterbridge training centre and turn right along the road. Take the next turn left to the main road by a lodge.

5 Turn right, up the road. After the entrance to Birkin House, bear left through a gate and immediately turn right on to a path through woodland, parallel with the road. Descend, cross a stile and bear left, signposted 'Higher Bockhampton', and inside the field bear diagonally right uphill. At the top corner keep straight on through a gate and follow the fence up towards a barn. Pass this and take a gate on the left and bear right on a track to the road. Turn left, then right by the postbox, and right again to return to the car park.

2 The Swanage Eccentric

See London architecture in a rural setting – and admire George Burt's clifftop 'folly'

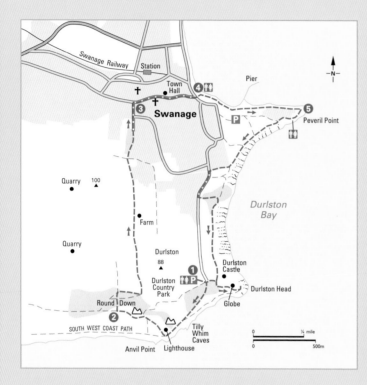

Distance 4.25 miles (6.8km)

Minimum Time 2hrs 30min

Ascent/Gradient 509ft (155m) ▲▲▲

Level of Difficulty ●●●

Paths Grassy paths, rocky tracks, pavements, 4 stiles

Landscape Spectacular cliff scenery, undulating hills, Swanage town

Suggested Map OS Explorer OL15 Purbeck & South Dorset

Start/Finish Grid reference: SZ 031773

Dog Friendliness Some town walking

Parking Durlston Country Park (fee)

Public Toilets Durlston Country Park; behind Heritage Centre on harbour (small charge); Peveril Point

1 Take the footpath directly below the visitor centre car park, signed to Tilly Whim and coast path. Steps lead down through some trees. With the sea ahead, follow the path round to the right, joining the coastal path. Keep right, towards the lighthouse, down the steep path. As you climb up the other side, look back and down to see the spectacular Tilly Whim Caves cut into the ledges of the cliff. Pass the lighthouse and turn right, then go through a kissing gate to follow the path with butterfly markers up the steep side of Round Down, with views to St Adhelm's Head.

2 At the top bear right, heading inland and parallel with a wall. Go down a slope, through a gate and across a footbridge, then turn up to the right. At a wooden gate turn left over a stone stile, following the butterfly marker. After another stile you can see the roll of the Purbeck Hills ahead and the roofs of

Swanage to the right. Cross a stile and go down a broad, grassy track. Beyond a stile by a farm this track narrows and begins to climb steeply. Continue straight ahead on to the road and follow this into the town, with the prominent church in front of you.

3 Turn right on to the main road. It's worth pausing to admire the little square with its butter cross and old stone houses tumbling down to the church. Continue along the street, but look out for: the modest metal plaque above the front door of No 82A, home of Taffy Evans; the elaborate Wesley memorial; and the extraordinary Town Hall with its Wren frontage.

4 At the square bear left beside the Heritage Centre, towards the harbour. Turn right and pass the entrance to the pier. Follow the fingerpost to the coastal path, then bear right, up the hill, past a modern apartment block and

a bizarre stone tower, to reach the tip of Peveril Point, with its coastguard station.

5 Turn right and walk up the grassy slope along the top of the cliffs. Take the path in the top corner and follow the Victoria's head markers to a road. Turn left through an area of pleasant Victorian villas. Erosion of the coastal path means a well-signed detour here, along the street, down to the left and left through a gate into woodland, signposted to the visitor centre and lighthouse. Follow the path for about 0.5 mile (800m) along the cliff top to Durlston Head. Pass Durlston Castle on your left and turn down to examine Burt's great stone globe. Stagger back up the steep hill to return to the car park.

3 Giant Steps to Cerne Abbas

Take a look at the remains of an ancient abbey before climbing to admire the famous chalk hill carving

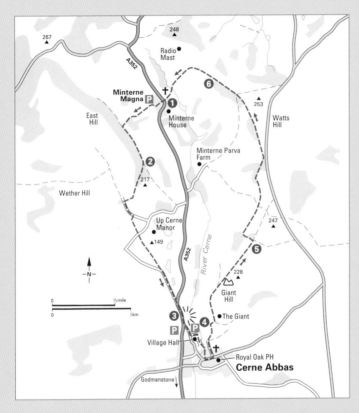

Distance 5.5 miles (8.8km)

Minimum Time 2hrs 30min

Ascent/Gradient 591ft (180m) ▲▲▲

Level of Difficulty ●●●

Paths Country paths and tracks, minor road, main road, 5 stiles

Landscape Head of Cerne Valley, scattered with old settlements

Suggested Map OS Explorer 117 Cerne Abbas & Bere Regis

Start/Finish Grid reference: ST 659043

Dog Friendliness Lead essential on road stretches

Parking Car park (free) opposite church in Minterne Magna

Public Toilets Cerne Abbas

1 With the road behind you, take the bridleway on the left side of the car park, which soon bends right and then left round some trees, and left again on the other side. Follow the track, keeping right at a fork, uphill, and where the hedge begins pass round to the right side of it. At the top, turn left on a track inside the woods.

2 Fork right down through the woods. At the bottom turn left along the road. After a bend take the footpath right, across the field. After a line of trees veer diagonally left, towards the right-hand of two white gates. Cross a road, pass to the right of this gate, and go straight on down the field, with Up Cerne Manor in view to the left. Pass another white gate to the right of a pond then turn left on the road. At the end bear right on to the A352.

3 Soon cross to the car park for the best view of the Giant. Fork left on the road down to the village and turn left, signposted 'Village Hall'. Turn right by the stream, signposted 'Village Centre'. Continue to the high street. Turn left, and left again in front of the New Inn, and left by the Royal Oak, to the church. Walk past the Old Pitchmarket to the Abbey. Turn right into the churchyard and bear left. Go through a gate and head left.

4 Cross a stile, then turn right up some steps. Now follow the path to the left, round the contour of the hill and past a National Trust sign for the Cerne Giant, below a fence. After 0.25 mile (400m), as the path divides, keep right, up the hill, to the top. Bear left along the ridge, cross a stile by a fingerpost and head diagonally right, to another fingerpost.

5 At the fingerpost turn left, signed 'Wessex Ridgeway', and go down through a gate. Soon turn right and follow the bridleway along the hillside. Keep straight ahead at a junction of tracks (signed 'Barne's Lane'), then dip down through a gateway and go straight on inside the top edge of some woods. Keep straight on to go through a gate near the road. Turn left away from the road (signed 'Minterne Magna') along the left edge of the large field. At a gateway turn left on to a gravel lane.

6 Directly above Minterne House, turn left through a small gate and signed 'Minterne Magna', towards the mast and follow fingerposts to the village, down through several gates and then along a broad track past the church to return to the car park.

4 A Dartmoor Outlier Above the Teign Valley

Enjoy wild daffodils at Steps Bridge, a magnificent view from Heltor Rock and the rood screen in Bridford church

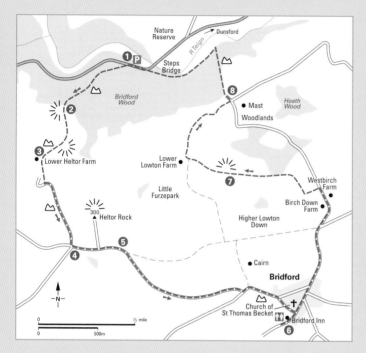

Distance 5 miles (8km)

Minimum Time 2hrs 45min

Ascent/Gradient 393ft (120m) ▲▲▲

Level of Difficulty ●●●

Paths Woodland paths, open fields and country lanes, 3 stiles

Landscape Steeply wooded valleys and undulating farmland

Suggested Map OS Explorer 110 Torquay & Dawlish

Start/Finish Grid reference: SX 803884

Dog Friendliness Keep under control at all times

Parking Free car park (and tourist information board) at Steps Bridge

Public Toilets None en route

1 From the car park cross the road, following the signs to the former youth hostel. Turn right up the concrete track, then left as signed towards the building; the path bears right, and is signed for Heltor Farm. The path leads uphill through oak then beech woodland. At the top of the wood cross a ladder stile as signed.

2 Follow wooden footpath posts straight up the field and through a small gate. Keep up the left edge of the next field; pass through a gateway and look left to see Heltor Rock.

3 At the end of the field turn left as signed through a wooden gate into a plantation; follow the path to meet a gate on to a lane. Turn left and walk uphill to meet a tarmac lane.

4 Turn left (signs for Bridford). After 200yds (183m) turn left over a stile up the narrow fenced permissive path to Heltor, from where you can enjoy an amazing panorama. Retrace your steps to the road and turn left.

5 After about 1 mile (1.6km) the lane bears left, then right, to reach the edge of Bridford. Turn right down a small steep lane signed 'Parish Hall & Church'. Follow church wall path, down steps and right to find the Bridford Inn.

6 Turn left from the pub and follow the lane through the centre of the village. Take the fourth turning (Neadon Lane) on the right, by a telephone box. Just past where a bridleway joins (from the left) the lane dips to the right, downhill; take the left fork and carry on straight ahead to pass Birch Down Farm on the right. Keep straight on again at Westbirch Farm; turn left as signed to Lowton Farm on a fenced path, which bears right to a kissing gate; pass through the gate and continue up the right edge of the next field to a stile in the top corner. Then cross over a tumbledown granite wall and carry straight on through an area of gorse bushes. Cross a stile by some beech trees.

7 Follow the fenced path along the top of two fields, and down a green lane to reach Lower Lowton Farm. Turn right as signed before the farm on a permissive bridlepath, which descends (with a stream, right) then rises to the next signpost; turn right for Steps Bridge down the narrow green lane, passing through a small gate. Continue down the deeply banked green lane until you reach a surfaced lane though a gate.

8 Turn left through the middle gate, signed 'Byway to Steps Bridge'. At the edge of Bridford Wood (by the National Trust sign) turn right following the footpath signposts. The path is fairly narrow and quite steep. Go left, then right, to cross a track, keeping downhill. The path drops down steps then runs to the left, now high above the river to Steps Bridge where it meets the road opposite the former café. Turn left here to return to your car.

5 Wartime Secrets at Inner Froward Point

Take in superb views of the sea and the offshore Mew Stone and discover the remains of military defences

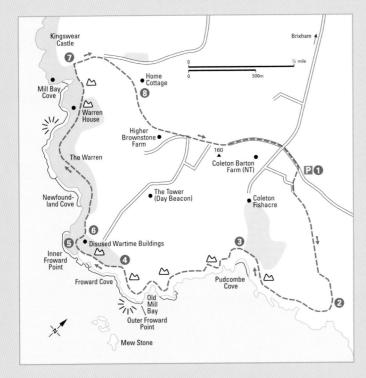

Distance 4.75 miles (7.7km)

Minimum Time 3hrs

Ascent/Gradient 525ft (160m) ▲▲▲

Level of Difficulty ●●●

Paths Varying coast path, tracks and lanes, steep steps, 7 stiles

Landscape Coastal cliff top and deep combes

Suggested Map OS Explorer OL20 South Devon

Start/Finish Grid reference: SX 910512

Dog Friendliness Dogs should be kept under control at all times

Parking National Trust car park at Coleton Camp

Public Toilets None en route

1 Walk through the kissing gate in the top right corner of the car park to take the National Trust's permissive path towards a metal gate and stile ('link path to Ivy Cove'). Keeping the hedge right, walk downhill to cross another stile, then another, and then another at the bottom of the field. Bear left to another stile. Continue uphill to reach the coast path (signs to Pudcombe Cove, right).

2 Turn right and follow the path along the cliff. Eventually go through a gate and descend steeply and over a footbridge to reach the gate at the bottom of Coleton Fishacre gardens. (There is no public right of way into the gardens here.)

3 Turn left, following coast path signs, to pass steps to the cove and go very steeply up wooden steps to leave the estate via a gate and on to Coleton Cliffs. The path drops

steeply, then climbs again above Old Mill Bay – with great views of the Mew Stone – followed by a steep climb up to Outer Froward Point, with views towards Start Point. The path undulates, then climbs steeply to reach the back of Froward Cove. Follow coast path signs left for Kingswear.

4 Pass through a gate, then follow coast path signs left, going very steeply downhill through a wooded section. The path then undulates towards Inner Froward Point.

5 The lookout (once housing a searchlight) is the next landmark, followed by 104 concrete steps climbing up the cliff. Follow the miniature railway line uphill and keep to the concrete walkway and steps as you pass through a collection of disused wartime buildings. At the top there is a junction of paths and a wooden footpath sign.

6 Turn left for Kingswear to walk through woodland behind Newfoundland Cove, through a gate and eventually a V-stile, and down a broad woodland track (estuary on the left). Plod down 84 steps to Mill Bay Cove and turn right down a tarmac way. Turn left over a stile and climb the 89 steps up to a lane, then 63 more steps to another lane.

7 Turn right (signed 'Brownstone'). After 250yds (229m) the lane forks; gratefully take the right fork downhill to Home Cottage.

8 Follow the footpath signs, right, up a steep, rocky path to a concrete lane, and on to pass Higher Brownstone Farm. Walk on up the lane to pass the National Trust car park, then the gates to Coleton Fishacre, and back to Coleton Camp car park.

6 The Bampton Notts

Follow part of the Exe Valley Way, with views of Exmoor, and explore Bampton and Morebath

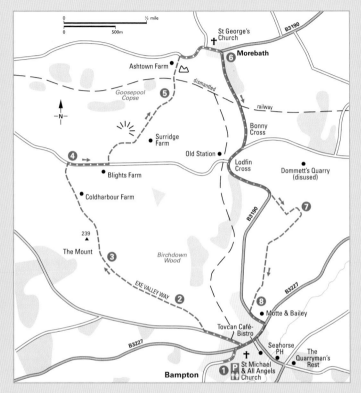

Distance 5.25 miles (8.4km)

Minimum Time 2hrs 30min

Ascent/Gradient 425ft (130m) ▲▲▲

Level of Difficulty ●●●

Paths Fields, tracks and lanes, 7 stiles

Landscape Rolling hills and wooded combes

Suggested Map OS Explorer 114 Exeter & the Exe Valley

Start/Finish Grid reference: SX 956223

Dog Friendliness Several difficult stiles; dogs to be kept under control

Parking Station Road car park by church in centre of Bampton

Public Toilets By car park

1 Leave the car park by the toilets, cross the road and turn left up the steep, narrow lane signposted 'Dulverton'. After a few minutes follow Exe Valley Way (EVW) signs right up a drive, left through a gate and up the field keeping right. Cross over the stile and go left on the track to reach a double stile in the top corner of the field. Over that, turn immediately right over another then turn left through a bank of trees and right, uphill (keeping the trees right).

2 Follow EVW signs over the next stile, carry on straight across the field to another stile (top left) and then cross the next field to an open gateway. Turn left, then immediately right, keeping the hedge on your left to reach a metal gate at the hilltop, with fine views towards Exmoor.

3 Continue downhill through open fields, with the hedge right, to reach Coldharbour Farm. Bear left before the farmhouse then straight on a grassy track, through a gate and downhill to reach the lane.

4 The EVW goes left here but the route turns right up the lane to reach Blights Farm. Turn left up the drive towards Surridge Farm. Just before reaching the farmhouse turn left through big metal gates, then another at the hilltop, continuing down through another gate on to a lane with views of Morebath ahead.

5 The lane joins a track; go downhill and over the dismantled railway towards Ashtown Farm, then right down the drive. Turn right and follow the deep lane uphill past The Old Vicarage to the centre of Morebath village.

6 Turn right down the B3190. At Bonny Cross keep right (signed 'Bampton'), past Lodfin Cross and the old station. When the road bends right take the track ahead, uphill.

7 At the hilltop a footpath sign leads right through a kissing gate. Go down the field, through a gate and over a stile, then straight on through a gate, over another stile, then through a gate at the top of the next field. Turn left through a gate. Cross the field diagonally towards the left-hand gate at the top. Pass through the next field to a stile at the top, then down a fenced path towards Bampton. Cross over the next stile and field to gain the road.

8 Cross over, turn left, then bear right down the old road into the town. Turn right towards the church and your car.

7 Dartmoor's Highest Tors

Enjoy superb views of Yes Tor and High Willhays on Dartmoor – without having to climb either of them

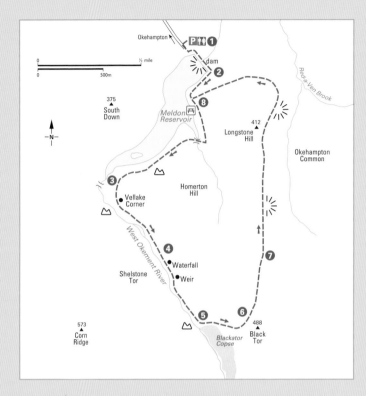

Distance 4.5 miles (7.2km)

Minimum Time 2hrs

Ascent/gradient 722ft (220m) ▲▲▲

Level of Difficulty ●●●

Paths Grassy tracks and open moorland, some boggy patches

Landscape Reservoir, ancient oak woodland and open moorland

Suggested Map OS Outdoor Leisure 28 Dartmoor

Start/Finish Grid Reference: SX 562918

Dog Friendliness Keep dogs under control, watch for sheep

Parking Car park at Meldon Reservoir (voluntary contributions)

Public Toilets At car park

1 Walk up the stone steps by the toilets, through the gate and go left on a tarmac way towards the dam, signposted 'Bridleway to Moor'. Cross over the dam.

2 Turn right along a stony track. You will soon see a gate (right) leading to a waterside picnic area. Don't go over the stile, but leave the track here to go straight on, following the edge of the reservoir through a side valley and over a small footbridge. The narrow path undulates to a steepish descent at the end of the reservoir to meet the broad marshy valley of the West Okement River; the swell of Corn Ridge, 1,762ft (537m), lies ahead.

3 Pass the small wooden footbridge and take the narrow path along the left edge of the valley, keeping to the bottom of the steep slope that rises on your left. The path broadens uphill and becomes grassy as it rounds Vellake Corner above the tumbling river below to the right.

4 At the top of the hill the track levels and Blackator Copse can be glimpsed ahead. Follow the river upstream past a waterfall and weir, go left of a granite enclosure, and along the left bank through open moorland to enter Blackator Copse – a wonderful picnic spot.

5 Retrace your steps out of the trees and bear right around the copse edge, aiming for the left outcrop of Black Tor on the ridge above. Pick your way through the bracken to gain the left edge of the left outcrop. The right outcrop rises to 1,647ft (502m).

6 Climb to the top of the tor if you wish; if not keep ahead in the same direction, away from Blackator Copse, aiming for a fairly obvious track visible ahead over Longstone Hill. To find it go slightly downhill from the tor to cross two small streams, then pass between granite blocks marking the track.

7 The intermittent track runs straight across open moor. Where the Red-a-Ven Brook Valley appears below to the right, enjoy the view of (left to right) Row Tor, West Mill Tor and Yes Tor. High Willhays, Dartmoor's highest point, lies just out of sight to the right. The track bears left around the end of the hill, with good views towards the quarry and viaduct, and drops back to the reservoir.

8 Bear right on the track, then left over the dam and back to the car park.

8 Merry Maidens and the Way Down to Lamorna

Step back into Cornwall's ancient past at the Tregiffian burial chamber and Merry Maidens stone circle

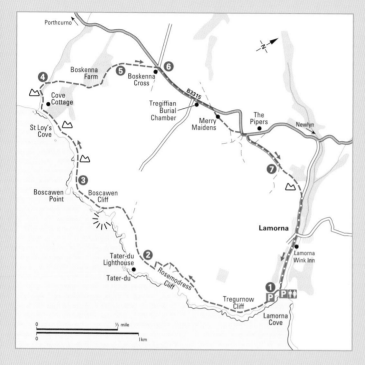

Distance 6 miles (9.7km)

Minimum Time 3hrs 30min

Ascent/Gradient 558ft (170m) ▲▲▲

Level of Difficulty ●●●

Paths Good coastal footpaths, field paths and rocky tracks

Landscape Picturesque coastline, fields and wooded valleys, 7 stiles

Suggested Map OS Explorer 102 Land's End

Start/Finish Grid reference: SW 450241

Dog Friendliness Dogs on leads through grazed areas

Parking Lamorna Cove or Boskena Cross

Public Toilets Lamorna Cove

1 From the far end of the seaward car park in the cove, above Lamorna Harbour, follow the coast path along through some awkward rocky sections. Continue on the coast path past the tops of Tregurnow Cliff and Rosemodress Cliff.

2 Pass above the entrance ramp and steps of Tater-du Lighthouse. Pass a large residence on the right and then, where the track bends right, keep left along the narrow coast path, at a signpost.

3 Descend steeply (taking great care when the ground is muddy) from Boscawen Cliff to St Loy's Cove. Cross over a section of sea-smoothed boulders that may be slippery when wet. About halfway along the beach, follow a path inland through trees and alongside the stream. Cross a private drive – Cove Cottage is just to the right – and then draw breath and climb steeply uphill. Go over a stile on to

a track, turn right over a stile and follow the path through trees.

4 By a wooden signpost and an old tree, go sharply down right and cross the stream on large boulders, then go left along a hedged-in path. In about 100yds (90m), go sharp right and up to a surfaced lane. Follow the lane uphill. At a junction with another track, keep going ahead and uphill. At Boskenna Farm buildings, follow the surfaced lane round left and keep ahead.

5 From the lane, at the entrance drive to a bungalow on the right, the right of way goes through a field gate, then slants diagonally right across the field to a wooden stile in a wire fence. Beyond this, the way (there's no path) leads diagonally across the field to its top right-hand corner, where a stile leads into a large roadside lay-by with a granite cross at its edge. An alternative to

the field route is to continue from the bungalow entrance along the farm lane, and then to turn right along the public road, with care, to reach the lay-by.

6 Follow the road to the Tregiffian burial chamber on the right and then to the Merry Maidens stone circle. From the stone circle, follow a grassy path towards a gate in the field corner. Go over a steep stile on the left, turn right aong the field-edge for about 55yds (50m) and go left across the field past a telegraph pole. Go over a stile on to a road, then go down the left-hand of two lanes, a surfaced lane with a 'No Through Road' sign.

7 Where the lane ends keep ahead on to a public bridleway. Follow a shady and very rocky track, that can be slippery in wet weather, downhill to the public road. Turn right and walk down the road, with care, passing the Lamorna Wink Inn, to the car park.

9 The Cornish Shores of Plymouth Sound

Take in beautiful river and sea views on this gentle circuit of the Rame Peninsula's eastern end

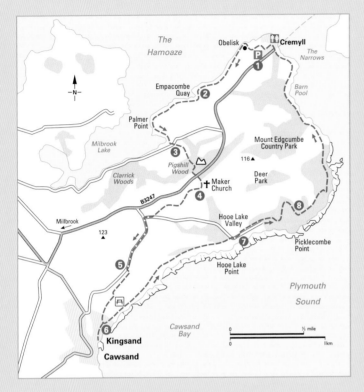

Distance 8 miles (12.9km)

Minimum Time 4hrs

Ascent/Gradient 328ft (100m) ▲▲▲

Level of Difficulty ●●●

Paths Good throughout. muddy in places in wet weather, 7 stiles

Landscape Wooded shoreline of tidal creek, fields, woods and coast

Suggested Map OS Explorer 108 Lower Tamar Valley & Plymouth

Start/Finish Grid reference: SX 453534

Dog Friendliness Dogs on leads through grazed areas

Parking Cremyll car park. Alternatively reach Cremyll by ferry from the Plymouth side. Daily service between Admiral's Hard, Stonehouse, Plymouth and Cremyll

Public Toilets Cremyll and Kingsand

1 Go left along the footway opposite the car park entrance. Where the footway ends at an old fountain and horse trough, cross back left and go through a gap by a telephone kiosk, signposted 'Empacombe'. Keep left past the Old School Rooms. Turn right at a junction then pass an obelisk and follow the path alongside the tree-hidden creek to Empacombe.

2 At a surfaced lane, by a house, keep ahead and go down to Empacombe Quay. Turn left beyond the low wall (dogs under control please) and skirt the edge of the small harbour to reach a stone stile on to a wooded path. Continue round Palmer Point and on to a public road.

3 Go through the kissing gate opposite, signposted 'Maker Church, Kingsand'. Follow the track ahead for 55yds (50m), then bear right, up the open field (no obvious path) heading between telegraph poles, and through a kissing gate into Pigshill Wood. Climb uphill following footpath signs. Cross a track, then go up some stone steps to reach more steps on to a public road. Cross, with care, and follow a path to Maker Church.

4 Turn sharp right in front of the church, follow the field-edge, then go over a stile on the left. Follow the next field-edge and cross a stile on the left, then follow the path past a house and across a lane into a field. Cross two fields to reach a lane. Turn up right, then go left at a junction.

5 Where the road levels off, bear off left down a track at a public footpath signpost. Keep ahead at a junction and, after a long level stretch, go left at a junction to reach Kingsand via Devonport Hill and Kingsway. To explore Kingsand and Cawsand, bear left down the narrow Heavitree Road.

6 To return to Cremyll, at Kingsway go through a gate into Mount Edgcumbe Country Park. Follow a good track to a public lane at Hooe Lake Valley.

7 Rejoin the coast path, signposted a little way along the lane. Keep to the upper path at a junction, then merge with a track from the left and continue through the woods.

8 Go left up some wooden steps, then zig-zag uphill to an arched ruin. Descend another set of wooden steps, cross a broad path by a gate, and zig-zag down through woods to the coast. Follow the coast path back to Mount Edgcumbe and Cremyll.

10 A Wild Flower Fiesta on the Cliffs at Bude

Marvel at the wild flowers that defy the battering of sea winds on Cornish cliffs

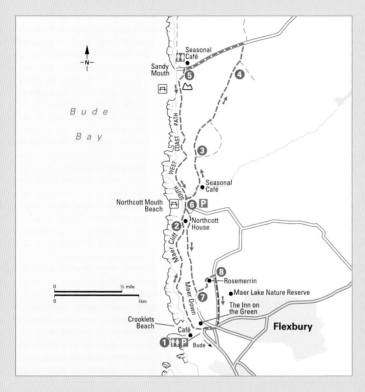

Distance 5 miles (8km)

Minimum Time 2hrs 30min

Ascent/Gradient 262ft (80m) ▲▲▲

Level of Difficulty ●●●

Paths Excellent throughout. The National Trust is carrying out regeneration of some eroded sections; please heed notices

Landscape Coastal cliffs. Keep well back from the cliff edges

Suggested Map OS Explorer 111 Bude, Boscastle & Tintagel and 126 Clovelly & Hartland

Start/Finish Grid reference: SS 204071

Dog Friendliness Dogs on leads through grazed areas

Parking Crooklets Beach car park. Follow signs for Crooklets. Large pay-and-display car park, can be very busy in summer

Public Toilets Crooklets Beach and Sandy Mouth

1 From Crooklets Beach car park, go towards the beach, turn right to cross a bridge and head for some steps. Pass behind some beach huts, then turn left along a stony track between walls. Go up some steps and on to the coast path, signposted 'Maer Cliff'. Follow the coast path.

2 Go through a gate and then walk along a track behind a white building called Northcott House. Bear off to the left, by a signpost, down a path to reach the sea at Northcott Mouth beach. From here, bear right along a track that will take you back inland, past a group of houses on the left, and continue uphill to pass some more houses.

3 Where the track bends right, leave it and keep straight ahead to an open gateway. Keep going along a banked bridle path ahead.

4 Reach a field gate and follow a track through the fields. At a junction with another track, keep straight ahead and continue to a T-junction with a public road. Turn left and walk down the road, proceeding with care on account of possible traffic, to Sandy Mouth.

5 Pass the National Trust information kiosk and descend towards the beach, then go left and uphill and follow the coast path back to Northcott Mouth beach, and a lifeguard hut passed earlier on your route.

6 Follow the roadside path just past the lifeguard hut and then retrace your steps towards Northcott House, which you passed earlier. Go along the track behind the building and then keep ahead along a broad track with a field hedge on your left.

7 As buildings come into view ahead, turn left over a stile with a footpath sign in a wall corner. Follow the field-edge ahead into a hedged-in path. Continue walking between trees to a lane by a house at Rosemerrin. Continue until you reach the road.

8 Turn right along the road, with Maer Lake Nature Reserve down to your left. Follow the road to a crossroads and turn right to return to the car park.

11 Cliffs and Deep Woods at Portreath and Tehidy

Combine steep climbs and clifftop vistas with a ramble inland past a farm and a golf course

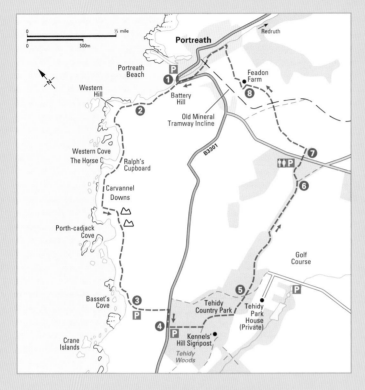

Distance 4 miles (6.4km)

Minimum Time 3hrs

Ascent/Gradient 459ft (140m) ▲▲▲

Level of Difficulty ●●●

Paths Good coastal path, woodland path, farm tracks

Landscape Precipitous sea cliffs and deep woodland

Suggested Map OS Explorer 104 Redruth & St Agnes

Start/Finish Grid reference: SW 654453

Dog Friendliness dogs on leads through grazed areas

Parking Portreath Beach, Basset's Cove, North Cliffs, Tehidy Country Park, East Lodge

Public Toilets Portreath and East Lodge car park

1 Cross the bridge opposite Portreath Beach car park and turn right up Battery Hill, following signs for 'Coast Path'. Take the lane uphill and carry on to where it ends at a section of houses situated above the beach. Then go left in front of garages, signposted 'Coast Path Gwithian'.

2 Follow the path through a gate and then keep straight uphill to the cliff top. Don't go too close to the cliff edge. Turn left and follow the path round the cliff edge above Ralph's Cupboard. Continue by steep paths into and out of Porth-cadjack Cove.

3 Keep going until you reach a car parking area above Basset's Cove. From there follow the broad track inland, then when you reach the public road, cross over and turn right for a short distance.

4 Turn left into a car park. Go through the car park and down a tree-lined track. Turn left at a T-junction and follow a track to another T-junction. Turn left along another broad track.

5 Reach a junction and four-way signpost beside two seats. (A café can be reached in 0.25 mile [400m] down the right-hand signposted track.) On the main route, keep straight on, signposted 'East Lodge'. Reach a junction by a seat. Keep right and go through a wooden kissing gate. Eyes left here before crossing to check for keen golfers about to tee-off. Go through a kissing gate and continue to follow the track alongside the golf course.

6 About 40yds (37m) beyond the end of the golf course section, at a junction, bear off left into woods. Stay on the main path, ignoring side paths, then bear round right to East Lodge car park and to a public road.

7 Cross the road diagonally right and then go left between wooden posts with red marks. Keep to the track ahead, pass chalets and reach a T-junction above farm buildings at Feadon Farm and the Duchy College.

8 Turn left, then in a few paces turn right down a concrete track. At a farmyard go sharp left by a public footpath sign and follow a path down through woods keeping to the main path, to reach a surfaced road. Just past 'Glenfeadon Castle' turn left along Glenfeadon Terrace, pass beneath a bridge, then at a junction keep ahead along Tregea Terrace and back to Portreath Beach car park.

12 Kilve and East Quantoxhead

With the risk of French invasion now passed, feel free to investigate these Tudor villages without fear of arrest

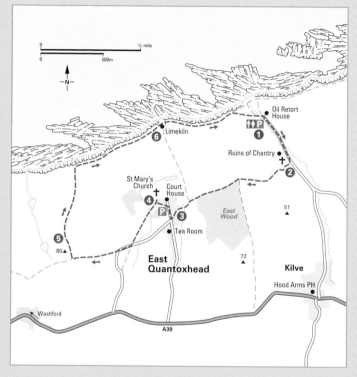

Distance 3 miles (4.8km)

Minimum Time 1hr 30min

Ascent/Gradient 250ft (76m) ▲▲▲

Level of Difficulty ●●●

Paths Tracks, field paths, and grassy cliff top, 4 stiles

Landscape Tudor villages, farmland and coastline

Suggested Map OS Explorer 140 Quantock Hills & Bridgwater

Start/Finish Grid reference: ST 144442

Dog Friendliness Extra care along cliff top, unstable near edge

Parking Pay-and-display at sea end of Sea Lane

Public Toilets At car park (closed October to February)

1 From the car park head back along the lane to the ruined chantry. Turn into the churchyard through a lychgate. Such gates were built to shelter coffins and their bearers: this one is too small for its purpose, so must be a modern reconstruction. Pass to the left of the church, to reach a kissing gate.

2 A signposted track crosses a field to a gate; bear right to another gate and pass along the foot of East Wood. (At its far end, a stile allows wandering into the wood, from April to August only.) Ignoring the stile on the left, keep ahead to a field gate with a stile and a track crossing a stream.

3 The track bends left past the gardens and ponds of East Quantoxhead to reach a tarred lane. Turn right, towards the Tudor Court House, but before its gateway bear left into a car park. Pass through to a tarred path and a kissing gate. In an open field this path bears right, to St Mary's Church.

4 Return to the kissing gate but don't go through, instead bear right to a field gate, and cross the field beyond to a distant gate and lane. Turn right and, where the lane bends left, keep ahead on to a green track. At its top, turn right at a 'Permissive path' noticeboard.

5 Follow field-edges, with hedges on your right, down to the cliff top, and turn right. A clifftop path leads to a kissing gate before a sharp dip, with a ruined lime kiln opposite. This was built around 1770 to process limestone, which was shipped from Wales, into lime for the fields and for mortar. The foreshore below the kiln is limestone, but it was still easier to bring it by sea across the Bristol Channel.

6 Turn around the head of the dip, and back left to the cliff top. Here an iron ladder descends to the foreshore: you can see alternating layers of blue-grey lias (a type of limestone) and grey shale. Fossils can be found here, but be aware that the cliffs are unstable – hard hats are now standard wear for geologists. Alternatively, given a suitably trained dog and the right sort of spear, you could pursue the traditional sport of 'glatting' – hunting conger eels in the rock pools. Continue along the wide clifftop path until a tarred path bears off to the right, crossing the stream studied by Coleridge. As you come into the car park, on your left is the brick chimney of a short-lived Oil Retort House (for oil distillation from the grey shale) from 1924.

13 Catching the Burrow Mump on the Levels

Taste the contrasts of the Somerset Levels before climbing the Burrow Mump

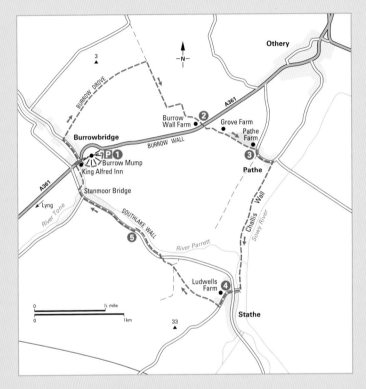

Distance 5.25 miles (8.4km)

Minimum Time 2hrs 15min

Ascent/Gradient 150ft (46m) ▲▲▲

Level of Difficulty ●●●

Paths Tracks, paths, unfrequented field-edges, 2 stiles

Landscape Flat pasture with ditches and one surprising, small hill

Suggested Map OS Explorer 140 Quantock Hills & Bridgwater

Start/Finish Grid reference: ST 360305

Dog Friendliness Good on drove tracks, where dogs are separated from livestock by deep ditches

Parking National Trust car park (free) at Burrow Mump

Public Toilets None en route

1 A gate leads on to the base of the Mump. Circle the hill's base to the left to a small gate and steps down to the Burrow Bridge. Just before the bridge turn right into Riverside. After 350yds (320m) turn right into Burrow Drove, which becomes a tractor track. On either side and between the fields are deep ditches, coated in bright green pondweed. At a T-junction there's a culvert of 19th-century brick on the left. Turn right here on a new track: it passes round to left of Burrow Wall Farm, to the busy A361.

2 A 'public footpath' sign points to a track opposite. After just 30yds (27m), turn left over a stile. With the bushy Burrow Wall on your right, cross a field to the usually muddy Grove Farm. Go through two gates below a wooded bank rising to continue along fields, to the right of buildings, on the left. At the corner of the second field a rusty gate leads up between brambles to a green track: turn right here to reach a lane near Pathe, a farm.

3 Turn right along the lane, ignoring a track on the right, to reach a side-lane on the right. Cross a bridge here to a hedge-gap on the right and a very narrow footbridge. Continue through several fields, with a wide ditch on the right. Near by, on the left, is the low banking of Challis Wall, concealing the Sowy River. The ditch on the right gradually gets smaller. When it finally ends bear right to the River Parrett and follow it to a latticework road bridge. Cross this into Stathe.

4 Keep ahead through the village past Ludwells Farm, to reach a kissing gate on the right waymarked 'Macmillan Way'. Follow the right edge of one field to a gatepost; cross to the hedge opposite and follow it round to the left, to a stile. Continue ahead with a hedge on your right, to where a hedged track leads to a road. Turn left, scrambling up the banking, to walk on the Southlake Wall between a road and river.

5 As the road turns away from the river, rejoin it. Once across Stanmoor Bridge you can bear right (if not too nettly) for a river bank path to Burrowbridge. Turn right across the bridge and, this time, climb to the top of Burrow Mump for fine views of Somerset.

14 The Villages of Hunstrete and Compton Dando

Enjoy a few hours' serenity in a rich landscape nestling between the busy cities of Bristol and Bath

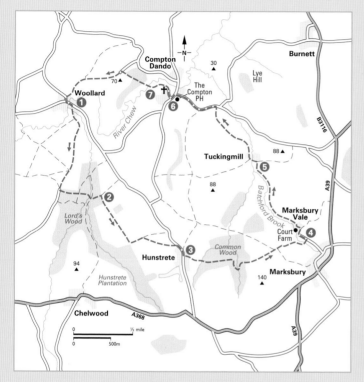

Distance 6.25 miles (10km)

Minimum Time 3hrs 30min

Ascent/Gradient 700ft (213m) ▲▲▲

Level of Difficulty ●●●

Paths Tracks, field paths, woodland paths and byways, 11 stiles

Landscape Rolling farmland with plantations and small streams

Suggested Map OS Explorer 155 Bristol & Bath

Start/Finish Grid reference: ST 632644

Dog Friendliness Freedom in some woods and on tracks fenced off from farmland

Parking Street parking near bridge in Woollard; also opposite pub in Compton Dando (Point 6)

Public Toilets None en route

1 From Woolard's crossroads take the road signposted 'Hunstrete' across the River Chew, then bear right at a 'Circular Walk' sign. The byway is underwater at first, but a path parallels it on the right. At the high point of the byway, where it becomes fully tarred, turn left through a gate into Lord's Wood. A wide path runs downhill, crossing a track, to a pool. Pass around to the left of this, to a waymarker and a track junction. The track opposite leads up to the edge of the wood.

2 Turn right, and drop to a hidden footbridge under trees. Head uphill, passing the right-hand edge of a plantation, to Pete's Gate beside a corner of Hunstrete Plantation. Turn left to a field gate. Turn right, around the field corner, to go through a gate. Continue along the same hedge, bending right at the field end, to reach a lane at the edge of Hunstrete.

3 Turn left beside Cottage No 5. Go down the right-hand side of a field to a stile into Common Wood. The track ahead passes through a paintball sports area. After it crosses a stream and bends left, take a signposted green path that rises to the top of the wood. Pass through a small col with a lone ash tree, and keep straight on, down across a field to a short hedged path. Go straight down the left edge of the field to a signpost, and turn right to join a lane at Marksbury Vale.

4 Turn left towards Court Farm; just before you reach the buildings turn right over a stile, and then follow the right-hand track for 100yds (91m) to a stile on the left. Pass to the right of the farm buildings as far as a rough track following Batchford Brook. After that head downstream until you reach a track at Tuckingmill.

5 Follow the track past a handsome 18th-century manor house to a ford. Cross the footbridge and turn right, alongside the stream, which is again the line of an underwater byway – rejoin it as it emerges. It leads to a road, with Compton Dando 700yds (640m) away on the left.

6 Turn right into Church Lane, and then go through the lychgate. A stile leads down steps, one of which is a 17th-century gravestone. Turn left behind the mill house and pass to the left of the mill pond, to reach a footbridge over the River Chew.

7 Bear left into Park Copse. At its top follow the right-hand edge of a field round to a stile. In the lane beyond turn left; it becomes a hedged track and runs past a tiny gorge as it descends to Woollard.

15 Salisbury's Historic Trail

Admire a wealth of architectural treasures dating back to the 13th century

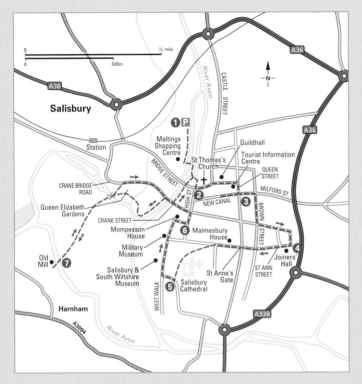

Distance 3 miles (4.8km)

Minimum Time 2hrs (longer if visiting attractions)

Ascent/Gradient Negligible ▲▲▲

Level of Difficulty ●●●

Paths Pavements and metalled footpaths

Landscape City streets and water-meadows

Suggested Map OS Explorer 130 Salisbury & Stonehenge; AA Street by Street Salisbury

Start/Finish Grid reference: SU 141303

Dog Friendliness Not suitable for dogs

Parking Central car park (signed off A36 ring road)

Public Toilets Central car park, Market Place, Crane Bridge Road

1 Join the Riverside Walk and follow the signposted path through the Maltings Shopping Centre towards St Thomas's church. On reaching St Thomas's Square, close to the Polly Tearooms, bear right to the junction of Bridge Street, Silver Street and the High Street.

2 Turn left along Silver Street and cross the road to the Poultry Cross. Keep ahead along Butcher Row and Fish Row to pass the Guildhall and tourist information centre. Turn right along Queen Street and turn right along New Canal to view the cinema foyer.

3 Return to the crossroads and go along Milford Street past the Red Lion. Turn right along Brown Street, then left along Trinity Street to pass Trinity Hospital. Pass Love Lane into Barnard Street and follow the road right to reach St Ann Street, opposite the Joiners' Hall.

4 Walk down St Ann Street and keep ahead on merging with Brown Street to reach the T-junction with St John's Street. Cross straight over and go through St Ann's Gate into the Cathedral Close. Pass Malmesbury House and Bishops Walk and take the path diagonally left across the green to reach the main entrance to the cathedral.

5 Pass the entrance, walk beside the barrier ahead and turn right. Shortly, turn right again along West Walk, passing Salisbury and South Wiltshire Museum and the Military Museum. Keep ahead around Chorister Green to pass Mompesson House.

6 Bear left through the gates into the High Street and turn left at the crossroads along Crane Street. Cross the River Avon and turn left along the metalled path beside the river

through Queen Elizabeth Gardens. Keep left by the play area and soon cross the footbridge to follow the Town Path across the water-meadows to the Old Mill (hotel) in Harnham.

7 Return along Town Path, cross the footbridge and keep straight ahead as far as Crane Bridge Road. Bear right, recross the Avon and turn immediately left along the riverside path to Bridge Street. Cross straight over and follow the path ahead towards The Mill. Walk back through the Maltings Shopping Centre to the car park.

16 The Longleat Estate

Drink in beautiful views from Heaven's Gate then wander the wooded arcadia of the Longleat Estate

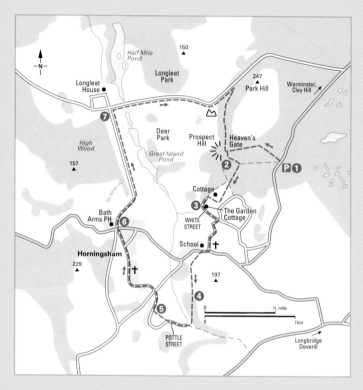

Distance 5.25 Miles (8.4km)

Minimum Time 2hrs 30min (longer if visiting Longleat attractions)

Ascent/Gradient 508ft (155m) ▲▲▲

Level of Difficulty ●●●

Paths Field, woodland and parkland paths, roads, 4 stiles

Landscape Wooded hillside, village streets, parkland

Suggested Map OS Explorer 143 Warminster & Trowbridge

Start/Finish Grid reference: ST 827422

Dog Friendliness On lead through grounds

Parking Heaven's Gate car park, Longleat Estate

Public Toilets Longleat attractions complex

1 Cross the road and follow the path into the trees. Disregard the straight track left, bear right and then left along a gravelled path through mixed woodland to double gates and reach the viewpoint at Heaven's Gate.

2 Facing Longleat, go through the gate in the left-hand corner. After 180yds (165m) at a crossing of paths, turn right, then keep right at a fork and head downhill through woodland to a metalled drive by a thatched cottage. Turn right on to the waymarked bridleway and pass the cottage gate. Now follow the path left, heading downhill close to the edge of the woodland to reach a lane running beside The Garden Cottage.

3 Turn left along White Street to a crossroads and turn right downhill. Ascend past the church to a T-junction and turn right.

Turn left opposite the school, following the bridle path up a track and between sheds to a gate. Bear left with the grassy track, pass through two gates and bear slightly right to a gate and stile on the edge of woodland.

4 Follow the path through the copse and soon bear off right diagonally downhill to a gate. Turn left along the field-edge to reach a track. Turn right, go through a gate beside a thatched cottage and follow the metalled lane (Pottle Street). In 200yds (183m), cross the stile on your right and cross the field to a stile and rejoin the lane.

5 Turn right and follow this quiet lane to a crossroads. Proceed straight across and follow the road through Horningsham village, passing the thatched chapel, and continuing as far as the crossroads opposite the Bath Arms.

6 Go straight across the crossroads, walk down the estate drive and through the gatehouse arch into Longleat Park. With the magnificent house ahead of you, walk beside the metalled drive with the lakes and weirs to your right. At a T-junction in front of the house, keep ahead to visit the house and follow the path left to reach the other tourist attractions.

7 For the main route, turn right and walk beside the drive, heading uphill through the Deer Park. Bear left with the drive and climb steeply, then turn sharp right through a wooden gate on to a metalled drive. With beautiful views across the parkland, gently ascend Prospect Hill and reach Heaven's Gate viewpoint. Retrace your steps to the car park.

17 Lydiard Park – Swindon's Surprising Secret

Take a wander around a Palladian mansion and country park on Swindon's urban fringe

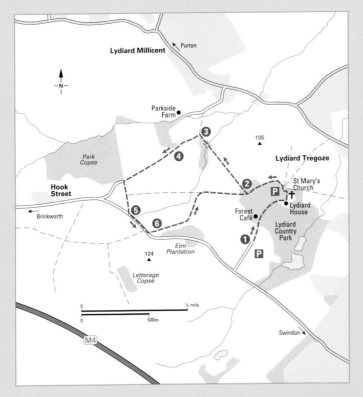

Distance 2.5 miles (4km)

Minimum Time 1hr

Ascent/Gradient 65ft (20m) ▲▲▲

Level of Difficulty ●●●

Paths Well-defined parkland paths and tracks, one stretch of quiet road

Landscape Farmland, parkland, woodland

Suggested Map OS Explorer 169 Cirencester & Swindon

Start/Finish Grid reference: SU 101844

Dog Friendliness Can be off lead in country park

Parking Free parking at Lydiard Country Park

Public Toilets Lydiard Country Park

1 Turn left out of the car park, pass the Forest Café and continue along the track to Lydiard House and the church. With the church on your right, bear left through the car park, ignoring the gate on your right, and go through another gate. Walk beside a walled garden and follow the path left into woodland.

2 Just before reaching a small clearing, turn right signposted 'Lydiard Millicent and Purton' to reach a gate on the woodland edge. Proceed straight ahead across the field on a defined path to a bridge spanning a stream.

3 Pass beneath electricity cables and turn left at a junction signposted 'West Park Circuit'. Follow the straight path with plantations to the right and at the next junction, with a path to Lydiard Millicent

on the right, turn left on the path marked West Park Circuit.

4 Keep woodland on the right and follow a broad track. Go through gates and continue ahead, avoiding a left-hand path back to Lydiard House. Keep ahead with hedgerow and trees to your right and at the first field corner bear right to the road at Hook Street.

5 Turn left, follow the narrow lane between fields and trees, pass under cables again and avoid a stile and footpath on the right. Turn left a few paces beyond it, through a galvanised kissing gate.

6 Bear right, following the field-edge, and make for a copse. Pass alongside it to reach a gate. Just beyond it turn left on to

a grassy path running alongside wire fencing. Follow it across a long rectangular pasture and swing right with the field boundary. Merge with a clearly defined track, with Lydiard House seen ahead framed by trees. Head for the clearing and retrace your steps back to the country park and car park.

Southeast England

There is an air of industriousness in Southeast England. Road and rail routes hum with activity and even the sky is seldom free from aircraft.

Yet amid the hustle and bustle there are green oases of peace and calm to discover, an immensely long and complex history to unravel, ancient ways to travel, mysteries to ponder – and the best way to see it all is on foot. This region boasts a gentle, rolling landscape with no towering heights, essentially agricultural but well wooded in places, threaded by a fine assortment of paths and tracks. Substantial areas of rolling downs and coast have been designated Areas of Outstanding Natural Beauty, and there is a network of long-distance walks.

If one geographical feature has shaped Britain's history more than any other, it is the English Channel. The white cliffs of Dover, the Seven Sisters and other chalk cliffs form England's southern bulwark. The eastern coast is altogether gentler and lower-lying, often crumbling into the sea – sand and shingle are constantly on the move. The Southeast's long coastline is rich in maritime history.

King's Lynn in Norfolk (see Walk 33) is one such example; first a small settlement called Lynn, it became a major centre of trade in the Middle Ages before attracting royal patronage, under Henry VIII. Sandwich in Kent (see Walk 24) has a proud history dating back to Saxon times as a major fishing and trading town, and became one of the 'Cinque Ports' in south-eastern England whose ships and men guarded the country against attack.

In Suffolk don't miss the idyllic Constable Country in Dedham Vale (see Walk 30), where you can stand in the very spot once occupied by English landscape artist John Constable when he created such masterpieces as *The Hay Wain*, *The White Horse* or *Boat Building at Flatford Mill*. In Norfolk, Thetford Forest (see Walk 32) was one of the first areas planted by the Forestry Commission after its foundation in 1919 and it now covers more than 50,000 acres (20,250ha). In Cambridgeshire you can visit one of the country's oldest nature reserves at Wicken Fen (see Walk 29), founded by the National Trust in 1899 but since expanded to 1,600 acres (648ha) and a haven for beetles and spiders, as well as many exotic plants including rare orchids.

Other parts of the southeast invoke a literary interest. Heading inland from the eastern coast, you can visit scenes from Charles Dickens' youth and old age in Rochester on the River Medway in Kent (see Walk 23). John Keats lived on the edge of Hampstead Heath in London after 1817 (see Walk 27). To the west of the capital, Pangbourne in Berkshire (see Walk 26) was a resort beside the River Thames in the early 20th century, when writers such as D. H. Lawrence visited. The Isle of Wight holds further delights for those interested in literature (see Walk 18). West Wight was home to English poet Alfred, Lord Tennyson from 1853 and at Farringford House or on the nearby down that today bears his name he wrote several celebrated poems.

At Beachy Head, the South Downs Way offers a fine route inland. On the South Downs you will encounter 'Glorious Goodwood' (see Walk 20) one of Britain's most celebrated racecourses. The course lies north of the Trundle Iron Age hill-fort (a vantage point for spectators) and on the estate of Goodwood House, home of the Duke of Richmond.

18 Tennyson's Freshwater

Tread in the poet's footsteps as you cross Tennyson Down and enjoy wonderful sea views

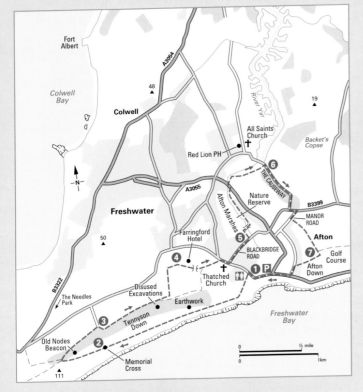

Distance 5.75 miles (9.2km)

Minimum Time 3hrs

Ascent/Gradient 623ft (190m) ▲ ▲ ▲

Level of Difficulty ● ● ●

Paths Downland, field and woodland paths, some road walking and stretch of disused railway, 4 stiles

Landscape Downland, farmland, freshwater marsh and salt marsh

Suggested Map OS Explorer OL29 Isle of Wight

Start/Finish Grid reference: SZ 346857

Dog Friendliness Let off lead on Tennyson Down and along old railway

Parking Pay-and-display car park at Freshwater Bay

Public Toilets Freshwater Bay and Yarmouth

1 From the car park, turn right along the road, then left before the bus shelter along a metalled track, signed 'Coastal Path'. After 50yds (46m) bear right through a gate and follow the well-walked path through a gateway and up to the memorial cross at the summit of Tennyson Down.

2 Continue down the wide grassy swathe, which narrows between gorse bushes, to reach the replica of the Old Nodes Beacon. Here, turn very sharp right down a chalk track. At a junction (car park right) keep straight on up the narrow path.

3 The path widens, then descends to a gate into woodland. Proceed close to the woodland fringe before emerging into more open countryside. Just beyond a disused pit on

your right, fork left at a waymark post down a narrower path. Cross a stile, then follow the enclosed path as it turns sharp left to a stile. Cross the next field to a stile and turn right along the field-edge to a stile.

4 Cross a farm track, go through a gate and walk along the track beside Farringford Hotel. Pass beneath a wooden footbridge and continue downhill to a gate and the road. Turn left if you wish to visit the hotel, otherwise turn right then, opposite the thatched church, turn left down Blackbridge Road. Just before Black Bridge, turn left into Afton Marshes Nature Reserve.

5 Join the nature trail, following it across a footbridge and beside the stream to the A3055 – this can be very wet in winter. Turn

left and almost immediately cross over to join the bridleway along the course of the old railway. In 0.5 mile (800m) you reach the Causeway. Turn left here to visit Freshwater church and the Red Lion.

6 Turn right and continue to the B3399, then left and shortly cross on to unmetalled Manor Road. In a few paces, bear left, signed 'Freshwater Way', and from this point ascend across grassland towards Afton Down.

7 Keep ahead at a junction of paths beside the golf course, soon to follow the gravel track right to the clubhouse. Go through a gate, pass in front of the building to reach the access track, keeping left to the A3055. Turn right downhill into Freshwater Bay.

19 A 'Testing' Trail From Stockbridge

Climb from a former Saxon stronghold to view an even older fortress – the Iron Age Danebury hill-fort

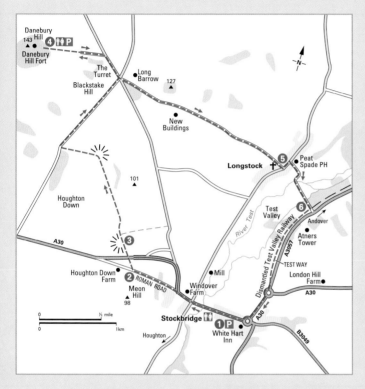

Distance 7 miles (11.3km)

Minimum Time 3hrs 30min

Ascent/Gradient 492ft (150m) ▲▲▲

Level of Difficulty ●●●

Paths Wide byways, field paths and railway track, 3 stiles

Landscape Open downland and river valley

Suggested Map OS Explorer 131 Romsey, Andover & Test Valley

Start/Finish Grid reference: SU 355351

Dog Friendliness Can run free on Danebury Hill (prohibited in hill-fort area)

Parking Along Stockbridge High Street

Public Toilets Danebury Hill (April to October) and Stockbridge

---

1 Walk west along the main street (A30), crossing the numerous braided streams of the River Test. Begin the climb out of the village and, just after the start of the dual carriageway, bear off to the left along Roman Road. Keep ahead at the end of the road, walking along the narrow defined path that climbs Meon Hill.

2 Just before Houghton Down Farm on your left, look out for a stile in the hedge on your right. Cross this and walk along the right-hand edge of a small orchard to a stile. Cross the A30, taking care, then walk through the gap opposite and along the right-hand edge of a large field.

3 Ignore the footpath turning on the right and keep to the main path, eventually bearing left with the field-edge to a grassy track leading to a gate and stile. Turn immediately right along a wide, hedged track and follow this for 0.75 mile (1.2km) to a junction. To visit Danebury Hill Fort, turn left towards The Wallops for 400yds (366m), then left again along the drive to the car park and access to Danebury Hill.

4 Retrace your steps back to the road junction you passed before Danebury Hill and take the byway to the left beneath a height barrier. Remain on this track as it descends back into the Test Valley. It becomes metalled as it enters the village of Longstock.

5 At the T-junction by the church turn left, then right beside the Peat Spade pub, along 'The Bunny'. Cross numerous streams that make up the River Test, notably one with a fishing hut and replica metal eel traps.

6 Just before crossing a bridge over the disused Test Valley railway, and the A3057, take the narrow footpath on the right. Drop down and turn right along the old railway trackbed (here forming a part of the Test Way) for about a mile (1.6km) to the A3057. Taking great care, turn right, walking along the roadside for 100yds (91m) to the roundabout, then follow the grassy verge to the next roundabout by the White Hart Inn. Turn right here to return to Stockbridge and your car.

20 Good Going at 'Glorious Goodwood' Racecourse

Try a country pub or a visit to an open-air museum on the way to one of Britain's best known racecourses

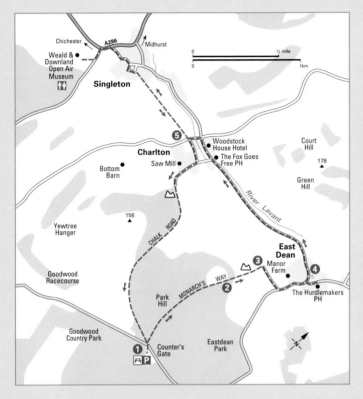

Distance 3.5 miles (5.7km)

Minimum Time 1hr 30min

Ascent/Gradient 328ft (100m) ▲▲▲

Level of Difficulty ●●●

Paths Woodland tracks and field paths, section of Monarch's Way and one lengthy stretch of quiet road, 4 stiles

Landscape Mixture of dense woodland and scenic downland

Suggested Map OS Explorer 120 Chichester, South Harting & Selsey or 121 Arundel & Pulborough

Start/Finish Grid Reference: SU 897113 (on Explorer 120)

Dog Friendliness Can run free on woodland tracks

Parking Counter's Gate free car park and picnic area at Goodwood Country Park or large free car park opposite racecourse

Public Toilets Weald and Downland Open Air Museum

1 Make for the western end of Counter's Gate car park and look for a footpath sign by an opening leading out to the road. Cross over to a junction of two clear tracks, with a path on the right. Follow the right-hand track, which is signposted 'public footpath' and part of the Monarch's Way, to a gate and stile. Continue to the next gate and stile and then cross a clearing in the woods.

2 Follow the gently curving path over the grassy, plant-strewn ground and down between trees to reach a gateway. Head diagonally right down the steep field slope to reach a stile in the corner.

3 Cross into the adjacent field and follow the boundary to a second stile leading out to the road. Bear left and walk down into East Dean, passing Manor Farm. Keep right at the junction in the village centre and, if it is opening time, why not follow the road for a short distance towards Petworth in order to visit The Hurdlemakers pub?

4 Leave East Dean by keeping the pond on your right-hand side and follow the road towards Midhurst and Singleton. On reaching Charlton village, pass The Fox Goes Free pub and the Woodstock House Hotel and take the next left turning. Follow the lane to a stile on the right and a turning on the left. If you are interested in investigating traditional village life at the Weald and Downland Open Air Museum at Singleton, cross over into the fields and follow the straight path. After your visit, return to this stile by the same route and take the road opposite.

5 Walk along to the junction and turn right by the war memorial, dedicated to fallen comrades of the Sussex Yeomanry in both world wars. Follow Chalk Road, which dwindles to a track on the outskirts of Charlton. Once clear of the village, the track climbs steadily between the trees. On the left are glimpses of a glorious, rolling landscape, while to the right Goodwood's superb downland racecourse edges into view between the trees. Follow the track all the way to the road and cross over to return to the Counter's Gate car park.

21 Devil's Dyke and 'the World's Grandest View'

See the views – as far as Haywards Heath and the Ashdown Forest – that Constable praised so highly

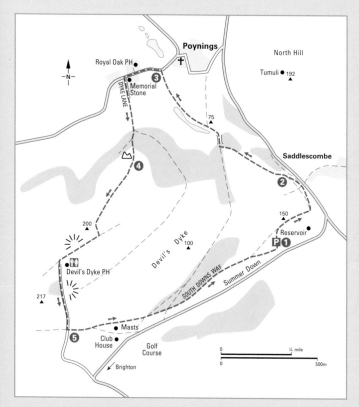

Distance 2.75 miles (4.4km)

Minimum Time 1hr 30min

Ascent/gradient 656ft (200m) ▲▲▲

Level of difficulty ●●●

Paths Field and woodland paths, 7 stiles

Landscape Chalk grassland, steep escarpment and woodland

Suggested Map OS Explorer 122 Brighton & Hove

Start/Finish Grid reference: TQ 269112

Dog Friendliness Mostly off lead. On lead on approach to Poynings

Parking Summer Down free car park

Public Toilets By Devil's Dyke pub

1 From the Summer Down car park go through the kissing gate and then veer right. Join the South Downs Way and follow it alongside lines of trees. Soon the path curves left and drops down to the road. Part company with the South Downs Way at this point, as it crosses over to join the private road to Saddlescombe Farm, and follow the verge for about 75yds (69m). Bear left at the footpath sign and drop down the bank to a stile.

2 Follow the line of the tarmac lane as it curves right to reach a waymark. Leave the lane and walk ahead alongside power lines, keeping the line of trees and bushes on the right. Look for a narrow path disappearing into the vegetation and make for a stile. Drop down some steps into the woods and turn

right at a junction with a bridleway. Take the path running off half left and follow it between fields and a wooded dell. Pass over a stile and continue to a stile in the left boundary. Cross a footbridge to a further stile and now turn right towards Poynings.

3 Head for a gate and footpath sign and turn left at the road. Follow the parallel path along to the Royal Oak and then continue to Dyke Lane on the left. There is a memorial stone here, dedicated to the memory of George Stephen Cave Cuttress, a resident of Poynings for more than 50 years, and erected by his widow. Follow the tarmac bridleway; soon it narrows to a path. On reaching the fork, by a National Trust sign for Devil's Dyke, veer right and begin climbing the steps.

4 Follow the path up to a gate and continue up the stairs. From the higher ground there are breathtaking views to the north and west. Make for a kissing gate and head up the slope towards the inn. Keep the Devil's Dyke pub on your left and take the road round to the left, passing a bridleway on the left. Follow the path parallel to the road and look to the left for a definitive view of Devil's Dyke.

5 Head for the South Downs Way and turn left by a National Trust sign for Summer Down to a stile and gate. Follow the trail, keeping Devil's Dyke down to your left, and eventually you reach a stile leading into Summer Down car park.

22 Great Dixter and its Gorgeous Gardens

Admire Great Dixter in the full beauty of its rural setting

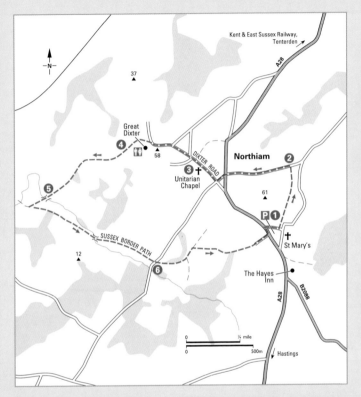

Distance 3 miles (4.8km)

Minimum Time 1hr 30min

Ascent/Gradient 98ft (30m) ▲▲▲

Level of Difficulty ●●●

Paths Field paths and quiet roads, 8 stiles

Landscape Undulating farmland and stretches of woodland

Suggested Map OS Explorer 125 Romney Marsh, Rye & Winchelsea

Start/Finish Grid Reference: TQ 828245

Dog Friendliness Dog stiles near Great Dixter and on Sussex Border Path

Parking Free car park on corner of Fullers Lane and A28, Northiam

Public Toilets Great Dixter, seasonal opening

1 Turn right out of the car park and walk along Fullers Lane towards St Mary's Church. Take the path on the left, signposted to Goddens Gill, and keep to the right edge of the field. Go through a gate in the corner and look for an oasthouse on the right. Make for a path on the far side of the field and follow it between fences towards a thatched cottage. Go through a gate to the road.

2 Turn left and head for the A28. Bear diagonally left across the A28 and follow Thyssel Lane signposted 'Great Dixter'. Turn right at the crossroads, following Dixter Road.

3 Pass the Unitarian Chapel and avoid the path on the right. Pass Higham Lane on the left and continue to follow the signs for Great Dixter. Disregard a turning on the right

(Dixter Lane) and go straight on, following a path between trees and hedges, parallel to the main drive to the house.

4 Pass the toilets and head towards a cattle grid. Cross the stile just to the left of it and follow the path signposted to Ewhurst. Follow the waymarks and keep the hedge on the left. Cross a stile in the field corner and then head diagonally down the field slope to the next stile. Follow the path down the field slope.

5 Make for a footbridge and then turn left to join the Sussex Border Path. The path skirts the field before disappearing left into some woodland. Emerging from the trees, cut straight across the next field to two stiles and a footbridge. Keep the woodland on the left and look for a gap in the trees. Cross a stream

to a stile and bear right. Follow the right edge of the field and keep on the Sussex Border Path until you reach the road.

6 Cross over the lane to a drive. Bear left and follow the path to a stile. Pass alongside woodland and then veer slightly away from the trees to a stile in the approaching boundary. Cross it and go straight ahead up the field slope. Take the first footpath on the right and follow it to a gap in the field corner. Cross a footbridge under the trees and continue along the right-hand edge of the next field to join a drive. Bear left and follow it to the A28. Cross over to return to the car park at Northiam.

23 A Dickens of a Walk at Rochester

Summon memories of *The Pickwick Papers* and *Great Expectations* in a tour of Rochester's characterful streets

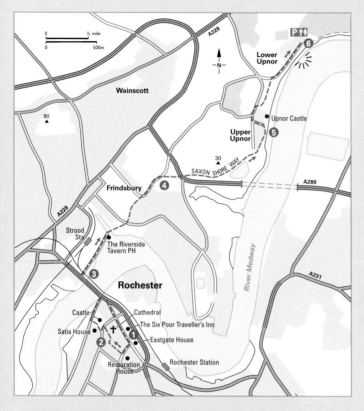

Distance 6 miles (9.7km)

Minimum Time 3hrs

Ascent/Gradient 98ft (30m) ▲▲▲

Level of Difficulty ●●●

Paths City streets and footpaths/cycleways

Landscape Historic townscapes and some rundown riverside sections

Suggested Map OS Explorer 163 Gravesend & Rochester

Start/Finish Grid reference: TQ 744685

Dog Friendliness Too busy for most dogs

Parking Blue Boar car park (fee)

Public Toilets At tourist information centre, also at Northgate

1 From the Blue Boar car park go left into the pedestrianised part of the High Street. Turn right up Crow Lane, then right by Restoration House into The Vines, a small park. Bear right half-way across the park, then turn right and walk down the hill to the cathedral.

2 Cross the road, turn left and walk round the castle. Pass Satis House, then turn right and walk by the River Medway until you reach Rochester Bridge. Cross the bridge and, at the traffic lights, go right along Canal Road, which runs under the railway bridge.

3 Walk along the river, pass The Riverside Tavern and follow the footpath sign. This brings you out to a new estate where you bear right along a footpath/cycle track, which is

part of the Saxon Shore Way. Keep walking in the same direction along this track, which is intersected by roads at several points. Watch out for the rusting hull of a ship.

4 At a bend in the road the Saxon Shore Way bears right, crosses industrial land and the A289, and then finally takes you close to the river bank again. At the river continue walking ahead as far as the entrance to Upnor Castle.

5 Turn left along Upnor's tiny, and extremely quaint, High Street, and then go to the right. Where a road joins from the left, keep walking ahead to join the footpath that runs to the right of the main road. Follow this to Lower Upnor, where you turn right to reach the quay and enjoy great views of the Medway. For even

better views, take a short detour up the hill to your left. Prehistoric wild animals once roamed these slopes, as archaeological evidence shows. One of the most interesting discoveries in the area was made in 1911, when a group of Royal Engineers working near Upnor dug up the remains of a mammoth dating back to the last ice age. It was taken to the Natural History Museum in London.

6 Retrace your steps back into Rochester. After crossing Rochester Bridge walk along the High Street, passing sights such as The Six Poor Travellers' Inn and Eastgate House, which is located beside the Blue Boar car park.

24 A Taste of Sandwich

Follow a gentle trail around this picturesque town

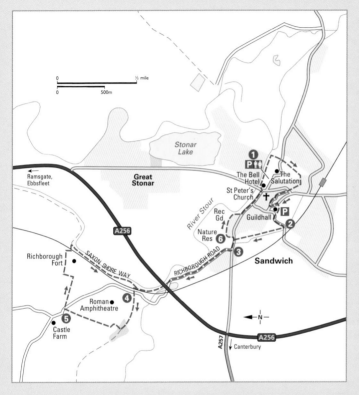

Distance 3 miles (4.8km)

Minimum Time 1hr 30min

Ascent/Gradient 98ft (30m) ▲▲▲

Level of Difficulty ●●●

Paths Easy town streets and field tracks, 9 stiles

Landscape Townscape, salt flats, golf course and beach

Suggested Map OS Explorer 150 Canterbury & The Isle of Thanet

Start/Finish Grid reference: TR 332582

Dog Friendliness Pretty good, can run free in some sections

Parking Car park (fee) at Sandwich Quay

Public Toilets New Street and the Quay, Sandwich and Sandwich Bay

1 Walk along the river bank away from the town, following the line of the old wall. At a bend in the river, turn right along a tarmac path to the road. Turn right, then left and continue along the path, passing the bowling green. Next turn right down steps into Mill Wall Place. When you reach the crossroads, go straight ahead along King Street, passing St Peter's Church, and then turn left along the intriguingly titled No Name Street. Afterwards cross New Street to the Guildhall, then walk though the car park and up to the Rope Walk, where rope makers used this long, straight area to lay out their ropes.

2 Turn right and when you reach the road, cross over and walk down The Butts. At the main road turn left, cross over and turn right up Richborough Road.

3 Walk ahead, past a scrapyard, and through a gate to join a footpath on the right. Follow the track round, under the main road and turn left to cross the railway line via stiles.

4 Cross the road, go through a kissing gate, then walk across the field to the trees, heading for the third telegraph pole. The path now goes into the trees: where it splits, fork right to a stile. Now follow the fence line and turn right at the marker beyond a ditch to reach a gate. Walk up the left-hand field-edge, cross a stile, go through a gate and cross a further stile to the road.

5 Cross over and walk up the track ahead. Richborough Fort is ahead. The track runs around the fort with expansive views over this seemingly endless landscape. At the

bottom of the track turn right along the end of a garden. Cross the stile and back over the railway, leaving it by another stile. The path now goes immediately right, over a bridge and back beside the river. You will eventually rejoin the road, and retrace your steps to the end of Richborough Road where you turn left.

6 Go left through a kissing gate, pass the Nature Reserve and go round the edge of a recreation ground. Bear right through trees and pass a car park to reach Strand Street and turn left. Go left in front of the Bell Hotel, and right past the Barbican and return to the car park.

25 The Puttenham Tales

Take a thought for pilgrims and others who have passed along what is now the North Downs Way

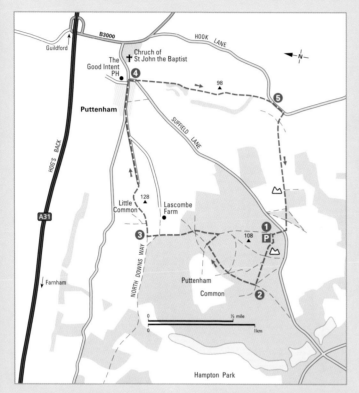

Distance 4 miles (6.4km)

Minimum Time 1hr 45min

Ascent/Gradient 295ft (90m) ▲▲▲

Level of Difficulty ●●●

Paths Woodland tracks and field-edge paths

Landscape Wooded heath and farmland

Suggested Map OS Explorer 145 Guildford & Farnham

Start/Finish Grid reference: SU 920461

Dog Friendliness Can run free on Puttenham Common, on lead in village

Parking Puttenham Common top car park

Public Toilets None en route

---

1 Head into the viewing area from the car park, dropping down into the trees with a wooden handrail running along on your right. Fork left through the woods, and bear right when the path forks again about 100yds (91m) further on. After 150yds (137m) cross another track at a clearing.

2 Turn right here opposite a green and mauve arrowed waymark post. Keep straight on until you reach another green and mauve banded waymark post 300yds (274m) further on. Fork right here, on to a narrow path that climbs gently through the bracken. Continue for 50yds (46m) beyond a line of electricity wires, then turn right, on to a broad sandy track. After 150yds (137m), turn sharp left on to a similar track. Pass a large red-brick house on your right, then, ignoring all turnings, follow the waymarked public bridleway all the way to the junction with the North Downs Way National Trail.

3 Turn sharp right here and follow the North Downs Way as it winds over Little Common and continues through Puttenham.

4 Turn right opposite The Good Intent, into Suffield Lane. As the lane swings to the right, nip over the stile by the public footpath signpost on your left, and follow the left-hand edge of an open field to the trees on the far side. Now take the waymarked route over a second stile to the left of the woods. Two more stiles now lead you away from the woods, keeping a post and wire fence on your right-hand side. Cross the stile beside a prominent oak tree and keep straight ahead, through the metal field gate. Bear right down a short, sharp slope towards the woods, and jump the stile leading out on to Hook Lane.

5 Turn right, and follow the road to the left-hand bend. Turn right again, over the stile by a public footpath sign. Two more stiles bring you to a right of way waymark; bear right here, and follow the post and wire fence on your right. Continue as far as a small wood, where you go through a kissing gate into an old sunken lane, and keep ahead for 150yds (137m) to a small waymark post. Continue straight on following public footpath signs to a T-junction with a public bridleway. Turn left and in 15yds (14m) turn right on a public footpath. Climb steeply here, for the short way back to Suffield Lane and the entrance to the car park where you started.

26 A Fashionable Riverside Resort at Pangbourne

Admire the gentle waters of the River Pang before heading for the Thames Path

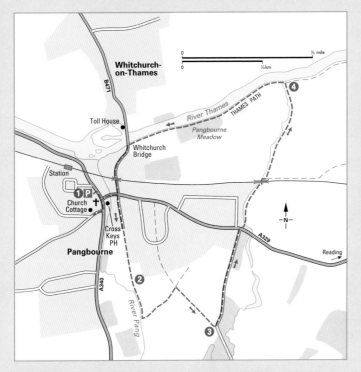

Distance 3 miles (4.8km)

Minimum Time 1hr 30min

Ascent/Gradient 220ft (67m) ▲▲▲

Level of Difficulty ●●●

Paths Field and riverside paths, stretches of road, section of thames path, 2 stiles

Landscape Gentle farmland on banks of Pang and Thames

Suggested Map OS Explorer 159 Reading, Wokingham & Pangbourne

Start/Finish Grid reference: SU 633765

Dog Friendliness On lead in Pangbourne, under control on farmland and by River Thames

Parking Car park off A329 in Pangbourne, near railway bridge

Public Toilets At car park

1 From the car park turn right to the mini-roundabout and walk along to the church and adjoining Church Cottage. Retrace your steps to the main road, keep the Cross Keys pub on the right and turn right at the mini-roundabout. Cross the Pang and bear right at the next major junction into The Moors. At the end of the drive continue ahead on a waymarked footpath. Pass alongside various houses and gardens and patches of scrub, then through a pretty tunnel of trees. Further on is a gate with a local map and information board. Beyond the gate the River Pang can be seen sweeping in from the right.

2 Follow the riverside path, with white willow trees seen on the bank. Make for a footbridge. Don't cross it, instead, turn sharp left and walk across the open meadow to a kissing gate in the far boundary. Once over it, keep alongside the hedge on the left and, as

you approach a Second World War pill box, turn right at a path intersection and cross a footbridge. Head for another footbridge on the far side of the field and then look for a third bridge with white railings, by the field boundary. Cross the bridge and the stile beyond it and then head across the field to the far boundary.

3 Exit to the road and bear left. Follow the lane between hedges and oak trees and walk along to the A329. Go diagonally right to the footpath by the sign for Purley Rise and follow the path north towards distant trees, a stream on your left. Through a kissing gate turn right at the next bridge and follow the concrete track as it bends left to run beneath the railway line. Once through it, bear right to a kissing gate and then follow the track along the left edge of the field, beside a rivulet. Ahead on the horizon are glorious hanging

woods on the north bank of the Thames. Pass double galvanised gates and a bridge on the left and continue on the footpath as it crosses this gentle lowland landscape. Go through a kissing gate and walk across the next field to reach the river bank.

4 On reaching the River Thames, turn left through a kissing gate and over a footbridge and head towards Pangbourne. Follow the Thames Path to Pangbourne Meadow and up ahead now is Whitchurch Bridge. As you approach it, begin to veer away from the river bank towards a car park. Keep left when you get to the road, pass beneath the railway line and turn right at the next junction. Bear right again at the mini-roundabout and return to the car park.

27 Spring has Sprung on Hampstead Heath

Explore one of London's best-loved open spaces

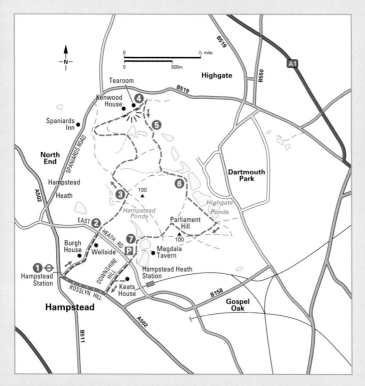

Distance 4.25 miles (6.8km)

Minimum Time 2hrs

Ascent/Gradient 344ft (105m) ▲▲▲

Level of Difficulty ●●●

Paths Mainly well-trodden heathland tracks

Landscape Heath and woodland scenery and some impressive views across London

Suggested Map OS Explorer 173 London North

Start/Finish Hampstead tube station

Dog Friendliness Keep dogs on leads near Kenwood House

Parking Car park off East Heath Road

Public Toilets Highgate

1 Turn left outside Hampstead tube along Hampstead High Street and left into Flask Walk. Continue down the hill past Burgh House and Hampstead Museum, along Well Walk and past Wellside on the right. Cross East Heath Road and continue along the Heath path.

2 Follow a tree-lined path past a fingerpost and a water tap and then after 100yds (91m) turn left at a crossing of paths by a bench. At a fork, bear left and soon afterwards turn right to go through a gate indicating the entrance to the 112 acres (45ha) maintained by English Heritage's Iveagh Bequest.

3 Turn left and bear left as the path descends gently through woodland. If you have a dog it should be on a lead now. Keep ahead to cross a bridge over a lake. Kenwood House can be seen over to the right. Turn left

and keep along a path that sweeps round, passing to the right of the house along a wide terrace that overlooks grassland. The Spaniards Inn is about 0.25 mile (400m) from here.

4 After passing the tearoom, take a left fork, signposted 'Kitchen Garden', to a pergola. Take a few moments here to enjoy the fine views over London, including the towers of Canary Wharf and the giant wheel of the London Eye. Next take a tarmac path to the right, which passes a metal gate.

5 Turn left, downhill, passing to the left of a lake and keep ahead through woodland. Look out for a metal gate on the right. Go through and then continue along the track ahead, taking the next left fork and heading uphill. At the next fork take the left-hand path, which then descends.

6 Pass three more ponds to turn sharp right after the last one, along a path to the right of a hedgerow that climbs uphill. At the next junction follow the right-hand path to the top of Parliament Hill where there are more views across London, including this time, St Paul's Cathedral. Continue ahead downhill along a path through the trees and between two ponds before heading uphill again.

7 Keep ahead as the path curves left and then bear right at a path junction, along a path to East Heath Road. Cross over into Devonshire Hill (turn first left into Keats Grove to visit Keats House), and continue ahead, turning right at the crossroads into Rosslyn Hill. Keep ahead uphill to reach Hampstead tube.

28 Stowe House and Gardens – 'A Work to Wonder at'

Savour the delights of a famous 18th-century landscape garden and surrounding parkland

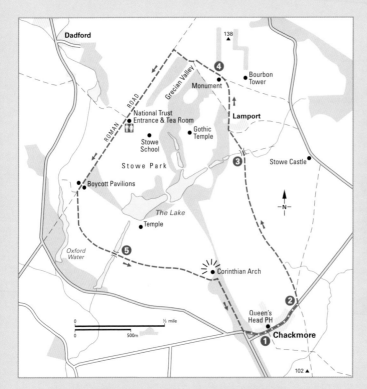

Distance 4.5 miles (7.2km)

Minimum Time 2hrs

Ascent/Gradient Negligible ▲▲▲

Level of Difficulty ●●●

Paths Field paths, estate drives, stretches of road, 3 stiles

Landscape Farmland and parkland

Suggested Map OS Explorer 192 Buckingham & Milton Keynes

Start/Finish Grid reference: SP 684357

Dog Friendliness Under control across farmland, on lead within Stowe Park

Parking On-street parking in Chackmore

Public Toilets Stowe Landscape Garden

1 Walk through Chackmore, pass the Queen's Head, and continue through the village. At the speed derestriction signs, keep ahead and look for a path on the left. Aim diagonally right in the field, passing under power lines. Make for a stile beneath the branches of an oak tree in the corner where waymarks indicate that the path forks.

2 Cross the field towards two stiles, making for the one on the left, beyond which is a plank bridge. Keep to the right boundary of an elongated field and when it widens, go diagonally right towards the far corner. Stowe Castle is over to the right, and to the left the outline of the Corinthian Arch is just visible among the trees. Through a gate join a path, pass under telegraph wires and look for a gap and waymark ahead. Walk ahead and then descend to the footbridge.

3 Go over the stream and through a gate into the field, then head up the slope, keeping to the left of two distant houses. Aim for a single-storey dwelling in the top corner and, as you climb the slope, the outline of the Gothic Temple looms into view. Go through a galvanised gate by a lodge at Lamport and continue ahead on the bridleway. The Bourbon Tower is clearly visible over to the right. Pass through a gate and keep ahead towards an obelisk monument commemorating the Duke of Buckingham. Merge with another path and keep a sports ground on your right.

4 Make for a gate leading out to the left of an avenue of trees running down towards the Grecian Valley. Cross over and follow the track on the right-hand side of the ha-ha up to a clump of trees. Bear left here and follow the wide avenue, part of a Roman road. Pass the

National Trust entrance building and shop and then the magnificent façade of Stowe School and keep along the main drive. On reaching the Boycott Pavilions, branch off half left along a track to a stile by the cattle grid and a sign for the Corinthian Arch. Down below lies the Oxford Water, crossed by a splendid 18th-century stone bridge.

5 Follow the drive through the parkland with glimpses of temples and classical designs. The drive eventually reaches the Corinthian Arch. Line up with the arch and pause here to absorb the breathtaking view of Stowe School, surely one of Britain's stateliest vistas. Walk down the avenue to the road junction, swing left and return to Chackmore.

29 Wicken – the Last Survivor

Step back in time to a piece of the ancient Great Fen

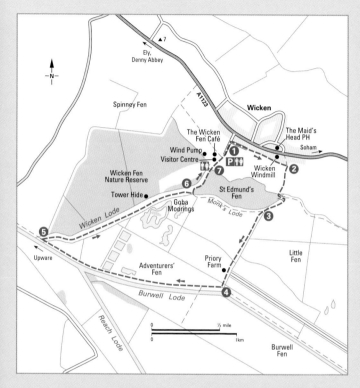

Distance 4.75 miles (7.7km)

Minimum Time 2hrs

Ascent/Gradient Negligible ▲▲▲

Level of Difficulty ●●●

Paths Mostly river banks and farm tracks, potentially slippery

Landscape Low-lying fenland of dykes, scrub and open fields

Suggested Map OS Explorer 226 Ely & Newmarket

Start/Finish Grid reference: TL 564706

Dog Friendliness Under close control due to livestock and nesting wildlife

Parking Wicken Fen nature reserve car park (pay-and-display) if visiting the reserve, otherwise off Wicken High Street

Public Toilets At nature reserve car park and visitor centre

1 From the nature reserve car park walk up Lode Lane towards the village of Wicken. Before you meet the main road turn right on to Back Lane and follow this route, which soon becomes a pleasant track running peacefully behind several houses. When you arrive at the far end of the lane, just after passing a windmill, turn right on to a wide track that runs across the fields. (If you have parked in the centre of the village you should take the signposted public footpath via Cross Green, just along from and opposite the pub, out to the fields.)

2 Follow this wide route down to two footbridges. Cross the second bridge and turn right along the bank of Monk's Lode, with St Edmund's Fen opposite. A lode, incidentally, is another name for an artificially cut waterway.

3 After about 550yds (503m), branch left before a fence and gate for a long straight track, known as a drove, and head out across the fields to Priory Farm. Join the surfaced lane and continue all the way to the end.

4 Turn right by the raised Cockup Bridge and walk along the bank of the Burwell Lode – don't be tempted by the footbridge. Continue for 1.5 miles (2.4km) past Adventurers' Fen, named after the 17th-century 'Gentlemen Adventurers' who first started draining the fens in earnest.

5 At a high-arched footbridge over Wicken Lode turn right and walk along this bank back towards Wicken Fen past a National Trust sign. If you continue across the footbridge and walk for another 0.25 mile (400m), you come to Upware, with a pub and picnic area.

Ignoring paths off into the open fen and fields on your right, continue along the bank until its junction with Monk's Lode. Across the water you pass the lofty thatched Tower Hide.

6 Cross the short bridge by Goba Moorings and continue alongside Wicken Lode, not along Monk's Lode (to the right). The lush vegetation of Wicken Fen is now either side.

7 When you get to the end turn left to the visitor centre (open daily from Easter to October, Tuesday to Sunday in winter). There is a small admission charge to the reserve itself, which is open daily from dawn to dusk. Nearby is the restored Fen Cottage, and a lovely thatched boathouse where the reserve's traditional working fen boat is kept. To return to the car park and village, simply walk back up the lane past the houses.

30 Constable Country at Flatford Mill

See Constable's studio and many of the scenes he painted

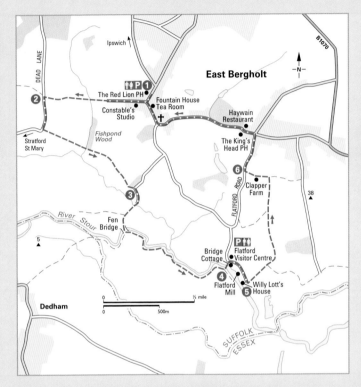

Distance 3.75 miles (6km)

Minimum Time 1hr 30min

Ascent/Gradient 246ft (75m) ▲▲▲

Level of Difficulty ●●●

Paths Roads, field paths and riverside meadows, 7 stiles

Landscape Pastoral landscapes of Stour Valley

Suggested Map OS Explorer 196 Sudbury, Hadleigh & Dedham Vale

Start/Finish Grid reference: TM 069346

Dog Friendliness Dogs should be kept mostly on leads

Parking Free car park next to Red Lion, East Bergholt

Public Toilets In car park and at Flatford visitor information centre

1 Turn right out of the car park, pass the Red Lion pub and the post office, then turn right along a lane, noting Constable's early studio on the left. Continue along this lane, past a chapel and a cemetery, through a gate and down the left side of a meadow to cross a footbridge. Climb the path for marvellous views of the Stour Valley and the church towers at Dedham and Stratford St Mary.

2 Turn left at a junction of paths to walk down Dead Lane, a sunken footpath. At the foot of the hill, turn left on to a field-edge path. The path goes right, then left to cross a stile on the edge of Fishpond Wood. Walk beside the wood for a few paces, then climb another stile into a field and walk beside the hedge to your right. The path switches to the other side of the hedge and back again before bending left around woodland to Fen Lane.

3 Turn right along the lane, crossing a cart bridge and ignoring footpaths to the left and to the right as you continue towards the wooden-arched Fen Bridge. Cross the bridge and turn left to walk beside the River Stour towards Flatford on the flood plain.

4 Cross a bridge to return to the north bank of the river beside Bridge Cottage. Turn right here, passing a restored dry dock on the way to Flatford Mill.

5 Walk past Willy Lott's House and turn left past the car park. An optional loop here, on a National Trust permissive path, leads right around the outside of Gibbonsgate Field beside a hedge. Otherwise, keep left on a wide track and go through the gate to join another National Trust path through Miller's Field. Stay on this path as it swings left and climbs

to the top of the field, then go straight ahead through a kissing gate. Keep ahead, ignore the stile on the left and follow a fenced path to a T-junction of paths. Turn left here along the track to the rear of barns and continue down the drive of Clapper Farm to Flatford Road.

6 Turn right along the road. At the crossroads, turn left passing the King's Head pub and Haywain Restaurant on the way back to East Bergholt. Stay on the pavement on the right side of the road to walk through the churchyard and back to the walk's start.

31 From Sunny Southwold and its Traditional Pier

Explore a charming holiday resort on an island surrounded by river, creek and sea

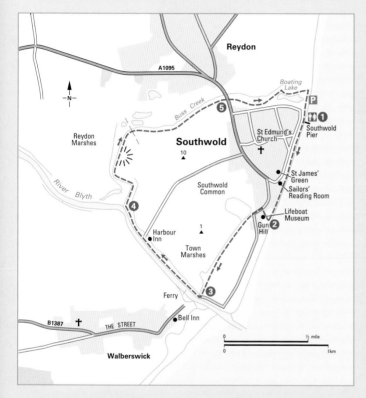

Distance 4 miles (6.4km)

Minimum Time 1hr 30min

Ascent/Gradient Negligible ▲▲▲

Level of Difficulty ●●●

Paths Riverside paths, seaside promenade, town streets, 2 stiles

Landscape Southwold and its surroundings – river, marshes, coast

Suggested Map OS Explorer 231 Southwold & Bungay

Start/Finish Grid reference: TM 511766

Dog Friendliness Most of walk suitable for dogs off leads

Parking Beach car park (pay-and-display) or free in nearby streets

Public Toilets Beside pier, near beach and car park at Southwold Harbour

1 Leave the pier and turn left along the seafront, either following the promenade past the beach huts and climbing some steps or walking along the clifftop path with views over the beach. After passing St James' Green, where a pair of cannon stand either side of a mast, continue along the clifftop path to Gun Hill, where six more cannon, captured at the Battle of Culloden near Inverness in 1746, can be seen facing out to sea.

2 From Gun Hill, head inland alongside the large South Green, then turn left along Queen's Road to the junction with Gardner Road. Cross this road, then look for the Ferry Path footpath, that follows a stream beside the marshes. Alternatively, stay on the clifftop path, and walk across the dunes until you reach the mouth of the River Blyth.

3 Turn right and walk beside the river, passing the Walberswick ferry, a group of fishing huts where fresh fish is sold, and the Harbour Inn. After about 0.75 mile (1.2km), you reach an iron bridge on the site of the old Southwold-to-Halesworth railway line.

4 Keep straight ahead at the bridge, crossing a stile and following the path round to the right alongside Buss Creek to make a complete circuit of the island. There are good views across the common to Southwold, dominated by the lighthouse and the tower of St Edmund's Church. Horses and cattle can often be seen grazing on the marshes. Keep straight ahead, going over a stile, through a gate to cross an embankment, then over another stile. Stay on the raised path to reach a white-painted bridge.

5 Climb up to the road and cross the bridge, then continue on the path beside Buss Creek with views of beach huts in the distance. The path skirts a boating lake on its way down to the sea. Turn right and walk across the car park to return to the pier.

32 Lynford's Stag and Arboretum

Tread the pine-carpeted paths of Thetford Forest

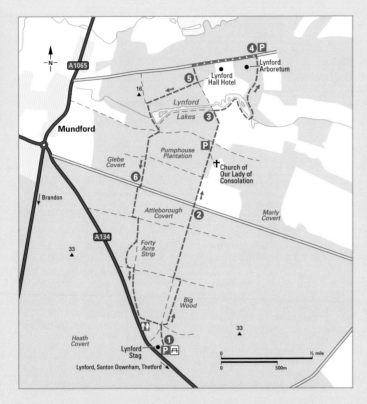

Distance 4.5 miles (7.2km)

Minimum Time 2hrs

Ascent/Gradient 66ft (20m) ▲▲▲

Level of Difficulty ●●●

Paths Wide grassy trackways and small paths

Landscape Coniferous and mixed deciduous forest

Suggested Map OS Explorer 229 Thetford Forest in The Brecks

Start/Finish Grid reference: TL 814917

Dog Friendliness On lead and keep away from children's play areas. No dogs (except guide dogs) in arboretum

Parking Lynford Stag picnic site off A134

Public Toilets Close to start

1 Leave the car park by the metal stag and follow the blue marker posts into the trees. Jig to the right and follow the markers north. The path then turns left; take the wide track to your right, next to a bench, leaving the blue trail to walk along the edge of the Christmas tree plantation until you reach a paved road.

2 Cross the road and continue on what was once part of the driveway leading to Lynford Hall. Pass a car park and a noticeboard with a map of forest trails. Continue along a gravel path, picking up the next set of blue and green trails. The Church of Our Lady of Consolation is behind the trees to your right. It was designed by Pugin in the 1870s for the Catholic owner of the hall, but the next owner, a Protestant, planted trees to shield it from view. Shortly, reach a stone bridge.

3 Turn right and follow the gravel path along the shore of Lynford Lakes with views across the water to Lynford Hall. Turn left across a bridge to enter Lynford Arboretum and follow the path through the arboretum until you reach a road.

4 Turn left along the road, passing Lynford Hall Hotel on your left. After you have walked past the building, turn left through the main entrance gates of the hotel and walk up the drive.

5 When you see a sculpture of two bulls fighting, turn right on to a wide grassy sward called Sequoia Avenue. Walk almost to the end of it, then follow the blue markers to the left into the wood. After a few paces you come to the lake. The blue trail bears to the left

at the end of the lake, but our walk continues straight ahead on the bridleway. The path jigs left, then right, but keep to the bridleway.

6 Cross a paved lane and continue straight on, towards the Christmas trees. Turn left at the end of the track, then almost immediately right, where you will pick up the blue trail markers again. Follow these until you reach the car park.

33 Fine Buildings in 'Lynn'

Wander cobbled lanes to visit King's Lynn's museums, see the river and take a ferry ride

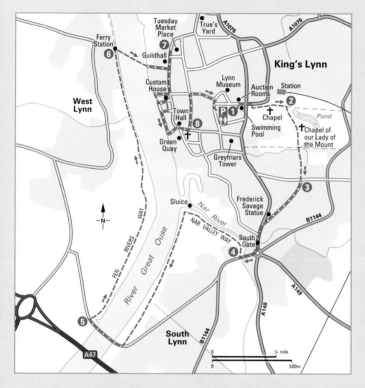

Distance 4 miles (6.4km)

Minimum Time 2hrs (allow longer for museums)

Ascent/Gradient Negligible ▲▲▲

Level of Difficulty ●●●

Paths Pavements, cobbled streets, grassy river path and steps to ferry (operates all year but not on Sundays)

Landscape Town buildings and open riverside

Suggested Map OS Explorer 250 Norfolk Coast West Ashdown

Start/Finish Grid reference: TF 620199

Dog Friendliness Dogs can roam free, but watch for traffic in town

Parking Blackfriar Street car park or St James multi-storey (pay-and-display)

Public Toilets At car park and various locations in town

1 From the car park, head for King's Lynn Auction Rooms, pass the fitness centre and swimming pool and cross the road to the park. Take the path towards the chapel of St John the Evangelist.

2 Turn right by the pond. On a little knoll to your left is the red-brick Chapel of Our Lady of the Mount, built in 1485 for pilgrims travelling to Walsingham. When you reach the ruinous walls of the town's defences, continue on the path straight ahead with the football ground to your left.

3 Keep straight ahead into Guanock Terrace, passing The Beeches guest house and Lord Napier pub to the statue of Mayor Frederick Savage. Bear left at London Road to 15th-century South Gate, then cross the road to the Honest Lawyer guest house. Walk past South

Gate and turn right at the roundabout. Cross a bridge over the River Nar and take the unmarked path to the right immediately after the bridge.

4 Clamber up the bank and take the path to the left along the east river bank. After 0.75 mile (1.2km), turn right over the bridge.

5 Turn right on the far side of the bridge on to the Fen Rivers Way. Follow this path for just over a mile (1.6km), with views across the river to King's Lynn.

6 Take the ferry back to King's Lynn. (The ferry runs every 20 minutes from 7am to 6pm, not Sundays.) Walk up Ferry Lane as far as King Street, then turn left to see the Tuesday Market Place with its 750-seat Corn Exchange concert hall.

7 Retrace your steps past Ferry Lane and continue to Purfleet Quay, which houses the Custom House. At the end of the quay, cross the bridge and take a narrow lane opposite to reach cobbled King's Staithe Lane. Turn right to return to the river bank, then head left to Thoreseby College, built in 1500 for 13 chantry priests. Turn left to walk along College Lane to reach the Saturday Market Place, with the Town House Museum to your left. Bear right and then left, passing the Town Hall and Old Gaol House, with St Margaret's Church dominating the square.

8 Turn left on to the pedestrian High Street for a flavour of the modern town. At the crossroads, turn right along New Conduit Street, then right on Tower Street. Take the alley to the left opposite Majestic Cinema to return to the car park.

34 Blakeney Eye's Magical Marshes

Walk along the sea defences to one of the finest bird reserves in the country

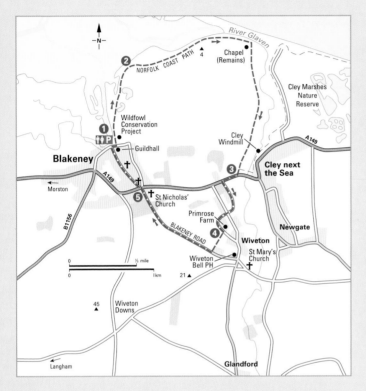

Distance 4.5 miles (7.2km)

Minimum Time 2hrs

Ascent/Gradient 98ft (30m) ▲▲▲

Level of Difficulty ●●●

Paths Footpaths with some paved lanes, can flood in winter

Landscape Salt marshes, scrubby meadows and farmland

Suggested Map OS Explorer 251Norfolk Coast Central

Start/Finish Grid reference: TG 028442

Dog Friendliness Under control as these are important refuges for birds

Parking Carnser (pay) car park, on seafront opposite Blakeney Guildhall and Manor Hotel

Public Toilets Across road from Carnser car park

1 From the car park head for the wildfowl conservation project, a fenced-off area teeming with ducks, geese and widgeon. A species list has been mounted on one side, so see how many you can spot. Take the path marked Norfolk Coast Path out towards the marshes. This raised bank is part of the sea defences, and is managed by the Environment Agency. Eventually, you have salt marshes on both sides.

2 At the turning, head east. Carmelite friars once lived around here, although there is little to see of their chapel, the remains of which are located just after you turn by the wooden staithe (landing stage) to head south again. This part of the walk is excellent for spotting kittiwakes and terns in late summer. Also, look for Sabine's gull, manx and sooty shearwaters, godwits, turnstones and curlews.

The path leads you past Cley Windmill, built in 1810 and which last operated in 1919. It is open to visitors and you can climb to the top to enjoy the view across the marshes. Follow the signs for the Norfolk Coast Path until you reach the A149.

3 Cross the A149 to the pavement opposite, then turn right. Take the first left after crossing the little creek. Eventually you reach the cobblestone houses of Wiveton and a crossroads; go straight ahead.

4 Take the grassy track opposite Primrose Farm to a T-junction. This is Blakeney Road; turn right along it. However, if you want refreshments before the homeward stretch, turn left and walk a short way to the Wiveton Bell. The lane is wide and ahead you will see St Nicholas' Church nestling among trees.

This dates from the 13th century, but was extended in the 14th. Its two towers served as navigation beacons for sailors, and the east, narrower one is floodlit at night.

5 At the A149 there are two lanes opposite you. Take the High Street fork on the left to walk through the centre of Blakeney village. Many cottages are owned by the Blakeney Neighbourhood Housing Society, which rents homes to those locals unable to buy their own. Don't miss the 14th-century Guildhall undercroft at the bottom of Mariner's Hill. After exploring the area, continue to the car park.

Central England

This region features many sites of national significance serving as both a centre of industry and 'the battlefield of England'.

People often think of the region in terms of simple images generated by names like 'the Potteries' and 'the Black Country' – as an area dominated by industry. For those interested in the country's industrial heritage there are certainly many sites to visit in the Midlands, including Coalbrookdale in Shropshire (see Walk 38), the place where the Industrial Revolution was born when, in 1709, Abraham Darby I developed a way of smelting iron with coke rather than laboriously produced charcoal. Within a century the locality was the world's leading industrial area.

Elsewhere in the region, Northamptonshire was known for its open-cast mining and Nottinghamshire for its coal fields. At Hartshill (see Walk 40) and Polesworth (see Walk 41) in Warwickshire and at Hereford in Worcestershire (see Walk 35) you can see parts of the canal network that supported industrial expansion.

The region's real upland wilderness is the Dark Peak, the wilder northern part of the Peak District – more specifically, the grough-riven blanket bogs of the Kinder plateau. This can be reached from the village of Edale (see Walk 47) in a steep climb up Jacob's Ladder to meet a section of the Pennine Way footpath. Elsewhere there are pockets of wilderness. In Cheshire, in an expanse of farmland, you can visit a fascinating section of lowland heath in the Little Budworth Country Park (see Walk 44).

The area also has also influenced many artists and writers, not least of course the Stratford-born poet and playwright William Shakespeare. You can walk in his footsteps in rural Warwickshire, perhaps make a visit to Kingsbury (see Walk 39), which has links with his mother Mary Arden, or stop at Hartshill (see Walk 40), which was home to his friend and fellow-poet Michael Drayton.

In Nottinghamshire the town of Eastwood was the birthplace of the major 20th-century novelist D. H. Lawrence (see Walk 48).

This is a landscape well fought over through the centuries. At the close of the Wars of the Roses in 1485, one of the largest armies ever assembled descended on Bosworth Field in Leicestershire so that rival claims to the throne could be settled. The same thing happened at Naseby, Northamptonshire, in 1645 only this time it was full-blown civil war. In the Second World War the Midlands suffered mightily. There are still military stations to be found in the Midlands – there are airfields along the Lincolnshire coast, for example, and near Gedney you can watch RAF planes from RAF Holbeach at their bombing practice over the sea (see Walk 51).

Despite the hard edges brought by canal, rail and road links, industry and urbanisation, and the feeling that the countryside exists only in thin strips alongside the Midlands motorways, there is actually a good deal of charming countryside to explore. Next time you pass through the area, turn on to the quiet by-roads, enquire into the heritage of the region and explore its hidden features. A little guidance is all you need in places where nature or history are not readily apparent, and you will find it a surprising and interesting experience.

35 Hereford's Lost Canal

Get a fascinating glimpse of Herefordshire history

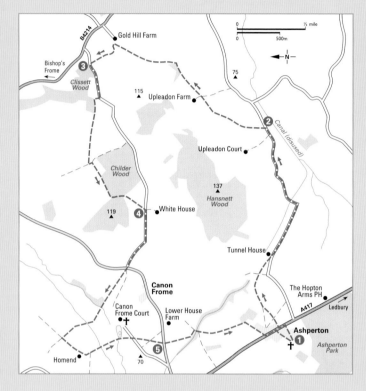

Distance 7.75 miles (12.5km)

Minimum Time 3hrs 30min

Ascent/Gradient 260ft (79m) ▲▲▲

Level of Difficulty ●●●

Paths Field and woodland paths, minor roads, at least 35 stiles

Landscape Gently undulating, mixed farming, woodland, derelict canal

Suggested Map OS Explorer 202 Leominster & Bromyard

Start/Finish Grid reference: SO 642415

Dog Friendliness Close control near livestock and on minor roads

Parking St Bartholomew's Church, Ashperton

Public Toilets None en route

1 From the church car park take the 'forty shillings' gate, behind houses, following waymarkers. Join a track to the A417. Turn left, then right, beside a high wooden fence. Follow a fingerpost across meadows for about 600yds (549m). Find a gate beside a cricket net. Cross the cricket field to a sightscreen, then a track, not joining Haywood Lane (to which the track leads) until some 250yds (229m) further, at the far corner. Turn left, passing Tunnel House. Continue for about 1 mile (1.6km). Find a stile on the left just beyond a gate about 100yds (91m) after the driveway to Upleadon Court.

2 Cross large arable fields and a ditch, then Upleadon Farm's driveway. Aim for the far left-hand corner, taking three gates, then skirt some woodland to your left, striking left (waymarked) at its corner, up a huge field. At Gold Hill Farm go right of a tall shed. Behind this, turn left, over two stiles. Turn right, ascending beside a wooden fence, but from its first corner follow a hawthorn boundary remnant to a road.

3 Turn left for 0.25 mile (400m). Where the road turns left go ahead, initially beside a wood, entering a huge field. Veer slightly left to find a (hidden) handrailed bridge with a broken stile beyond it. Turn left but in 25yds (23m) turn right, before a gate. After 500yds (457m) enter trees. On leaving them strike half right for the large White House.

4 Turn right along the road. When you reach the junction, take the footpath opposite, across a long field. Beyond some trees, aim right of a solitary oak. Walk across fields, over three footbridges and under power lines, passing through a gap to another stile, but do not cross this – note three waymarkers on its far side. Turn left. Just beyond Homend find a stile in a far left-hand corner of an old orchard, shielded by an ash and a larch. Turn left, soon moving right to double gates flanking a wide concrete bridge. After the leafy avenue keep ahead, veering right when a pond is behind trees to your left. Cross the driveway to Canon Frome Court, then another track, finally reaching a road by a spinney.

5 Cross over the road and walk straight to the canal. Turn left. In 140yds (128m) turn right, over the canal. Veer left and uphill, finding a large oak in the top left-hand corner. Keep this line despite the field boundary curving away. On reaching a copse turn right, later moving left into an indistinct lane. The village hall heralds the A417. Turn left, along the pavement, then right to the church.

36 Follow the Buzzard to the Heights of Bury Ditches

Enjoy magnificent views from a dramatic hill-fort

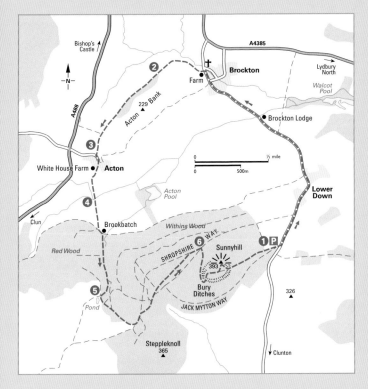

Distance 5.5 miles (8.8km)

Minimum Time 2hrs

Ascent/Gradient 804ft (245m) ▲▲▲

Level of Difficulty ●●●

Paths Field and woodland paths, one boggy and overgrown, fence and gates to climb at Acton Bank, 8 stiles

Landscape Hilltop woodland and plantation, mixed farmland in valley

Suggested Map OS Explorer 216 Welshpool & Montgomery

Start/Finish Grid reference: SO 334839

Dog Friendliness Off lead for much of way, but not round Acton

Parking Forestry Commission car park at Sunnyhill off minor road north from Clunton

Public Toilets None en route

1 From the car park at Sunnyhill, walk back to the lane and turn left. Descend through Lower Down to Brockton. Turn left on a track shortly before you come to a ford. Pass a collection of buses in a yard, then go through a gate on the left and walk along the right-hand edges of three fields, parallel with the track.

2 Climb over a fence into a wood then join the track just below, contouring round the base of Acton Bank. After leaving the wood the path continues through scrub, then through pasture below some old quarries, before it meets a lane at the hamlet of Acton.

3 Turn left, pass to the right of a triangular green and join a path past White House Farm. Frequent waymarkers guide you past the house, across a field, then left over a stile and along the right-hand edge of another field.

4 Cross a footbridge and continue straight across the field towards a building at the far side. Cross a stile in the hedge, turn left for a few paces then right on a track that passes by a house called Brookbatch on your left and into woodland. When the track bends to the left, go over a stile instead and then continue climbing.

5 Emerging on to a track, turn left past a pond on your right. Cross a defunct cattle grid into Forestry Commission property and leave the track, turning right on a footpath through beechwoods. At a crossroads of tracks turn left, then bear right on a forestry track by a Shropshire Way sign. Ignore all side turnings until the Shropshire Way goes left at a fork.

6 Climb gently for a while. Where the main track levels off and starts to descend, turn right. The path leads to Bury Ditches hill fort, then cuts through a gap in the ramparts and crosses the interior. At a colour-banded post (red, blue and green), a path branches left to allow a visit to the summit, with marvellous views. Bear right to return to the main path and turn left to follow it to the car park.

37 Gone to Earth on Lovely Lyth Hill

Savour the panoramic views that gave inspiration to the novelist Mary Webb

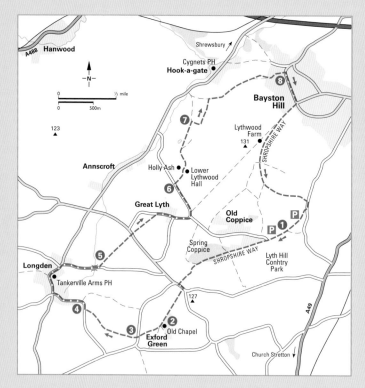

Distance 7.75 miles (12.5km)

Minimum Time 3hrs

Ascent/Gradient 500ft (152m) ▲▲▲

Level of Difficulty ●●●

Paths Cross-field paths, mostly well-maintained, about 30 stiles

Landscape Rolling farmland and views from Lyth Hill's grassy top

Suggested Map OS Explorer 241 Shrewsbury

Start/Finish Grid reference: SJ 473069

Dog Friendliness Must be on lead near livestock, also at Exford Green

Parking Car park in country park at top of Lyth Hill (signposted)

Public Toilets None en route

1 Head southwest on the Shropshire Way. Ignore a path branching right into Spring Coppice. The Way descends to a track. Follow this past The Yews to a lane, where you turn left, then first right, on a track to Exford Green.

2 Cross two stiles to skirt a former Primitive Methodist chapel. Leave the Shropshire Way, going diagonally across a field, heading for the far corner. Cross a stile close to the corner and go through a copse to reach a lane.

3 Cross to a path almost opposite, following the left-hand edge of a field until you come to a stile that gives access to another. Head diagonally across to a point close to the far right corner. Cross a stile and continue across another field, past two oak trees. A worn path goes obliquely right across the next two fields to meet a lane.

4 Turn right, then right again at the main road. Pass through Longden. Go right again on School Lane; this descends very slightly. Cross a brook, then go through a gate on the left and diagonally right across a field corner to a stile.

5 A yellow arrow directs you diagonally across the next field to a stile under an oak tree between two telegraph posts. Cross another field to reach a road. The path continues opposite, crossing two further fields until it meets a lane at Great Lyth. Turn right on the lane, keeping straight on at a junction, then turn left at the next.

6 Turn right on the access track to Lower Lythwood Hall and Holly Ash. At the end, turn left on a lush green lane. At its end turn right over a stile and cross a field. Pass a row

of three oak trees, then keep to the right of a pond to reach a stile at the far side. Follow the edge of the next field to a gate. Continue along a track for a few paces until you can cross a stile on the right.

7 Walk up the right edge of the field and turn left along the top. Follow a worn path across a field, go through a kissing gate, and along field-edges to a path behind houses.

8 Meeting a street, turn immediately right on a fenced path, then straight ahead on a street. Turn right then first left (Bredden Way). At the top turn right then left by a postbox through trees to a lane. Turn right to Lythwood Farm. Go straight through then fork left and follow the track across fields. Cross the last field aiming left of a small reservoir. Emerge to a lane and turn right, back to Lyth Hill.

42 A Rutland Waterside Walk

Wander the shore of England's largest expanse of inland water

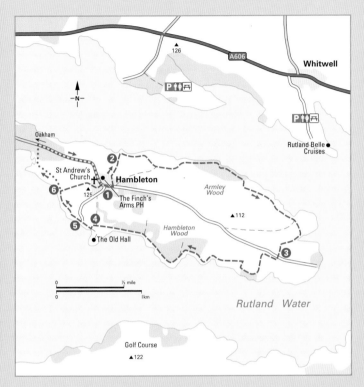

Distance 4.5 miles (7.2km)

Minimum Time 2hrs

Ascent/Gradient 311ft (95m) ▲▲▲

Level of Difficulty ●●●

Paths Wide and firm the whole distance, 3 stiles

Landscape Low-lying peninsula of dipping fields and woodland

Suggested Map OS Explorer 234 Rutland Water

Start/Finish Grid reference: SK 900075

Dog Friendliness On lead in fields of stock and around nesting birds

Parking Roadside parking in Hambleton

Public Toilets None en route (nearest in Oakham)

1 From St Andrew's Church in the centre of the village of Hambleton, walk eastwards on the long main street as far as the red pillar box. Turn left opposite the pillar box on a wide track indicated 'public footpath' that leads straight through a gate and down the middle of a sloping field.

2 Go through the gate at the bottom of the field and turn right on to the wide track that runs just above the shore. This popular and peaceful route around the Hambleton peninsula is shared with cyclists, so enjoy the walk, but be alert. Follow it from field to field, and through Armley Wood, with ever-changing views across Rutland Water. As you gradually swing around the tip of the Hambleton peninsula with views towards the dam at the eastern end, you can begin to appreciate the sheer size of the reservoir.

3 When you arrive at a tarmac lane – which is gated to traffic at this point, since it disappears into the water a little further on! – go straight across to continue on the same unmade track. It turns right and runs parallel with the road a short distance, before heading left and back towards the water's edge and a section of mixed woodland. Continue by the lakeside for just over 1 mile (1.6km).

4 Approaching The Old Hall, a handsome building perched just above the shore, turn left to reach its surfaced drive, then go right and walk along it for 160yds (146m) to reach a cattle grid.

5 At this point you can, if you wish, return directly to Hambleton by following the lane back uphill; otherwise veer left to continue along the open, waterside track, with

views across to Egleton Bay and the corner of Rutland Water specially reserved for wildlife – it's out of bounds to sailing boats.

6 After about 500yds (457m) look for the easily missed stile in the hedge on your right, and the public footpath that heads straight up the field. If you overshoot, or want to extend the walk by 0.5 mile (800m), simply carry on along the track to the very far end and return along the lane to the village. Aim for the apex of the field, where successive stiles lead to a narrow passageway between a hedge and a fence that eventually brings you out in the churchyard in the centre of the village.

43 Castle Ashby and its Estate

Take a turn around an estate once graced by royalty

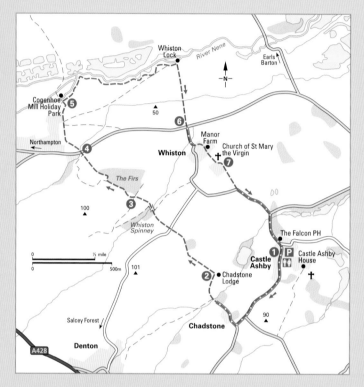

Distance 6.5 miles (10.4km)

Minimum Time 3hrs

Ascent/Gradient 557ft (170m) ▲▲▲

Level of Difficulty ●●●

Paths Field paths, farm tracks and river bank, some steps

Landscape Low rolling hills above gentle Nene Valley

Suggested Map OS Explorer 207 Newport Pagnell & Northampton South

Start/Finish Grid reference: SP 859594

Dog Friendliness Mostly arable fields, so generally good

Parking Roadside in Castle Ashby, or car park for visitors

Public Toilets Rural Shopping Yard, Castle Ashby

1 Walk out of Castle Ashby along the road heading southwestwards, with the house (and visitors' car park) over to your left. Where the pavement ends turn right for Chadstone. Drop down the lane past the cottages and expensive-looking converted barns and continue all the way out of the hamlet to the farm of Chadstone Lodge.

2 Turn left for the bridleway behind the hedge and, at the end of the bridleway, go on through the trees to continue the route alongside the next field and on down to a road. Cross over for a footpath opposite that leads down to Whiston Spinney, then continue via a footbridge through a lovely shady dell until you reach a junction of tracks on the far side. At this point continue straight on, and then climb directly up the sloping field ahead towards the trees on the far side.

3 Follow the path into the woods to climb some steps and head out along a field-edge with woodland on your right. Beyond a gate go down a sharp flight of steps to the right and across a field in order to turn left on the far side and drop down to the road below.

4 The route continues up through the field opposite. Head half left, then follow the bridleway waymarks to the right, through a long narrow field with the houses of Cogenhoe on your left. At the far side join a lane and descend to Cogenhoe Mill.

5 Just before the old mill buildings and sluice, with the holiday park beyond, turn right for a path alongside the River Nene (signposted 'Nene Way'). Follow this pleasant waterside walk for 1 mile (1.6km) as far as Whiston Lock, then turn right for a straight farm track across the fields to the main road, heading towards Whiston church sitting astride the hilltop like a lighthouse.

6 Go across the junction and walk along the lane into Whiston, branching left at the small triangular village green. Take the gated passageway beside the outbuildings of Manor Farm and continue up towards the church. There are good views across the Nene Valley to Earls Barton and Wellingborough, and the eastern edge of Northampton.

7 Walk past the church to the far side of the churchyard, go over a metal rung in the wall and turn right on to an obvious field-edge path. This continues along a grassy strip between further fields and emerges on to the bend of a lane. Go straight on/left to walk this all the way back to Castle Ashby.

44 Woods and Heaths of Little Budworth

Take your chance to see the fascinating wildlife in a rare piece of lowland heath

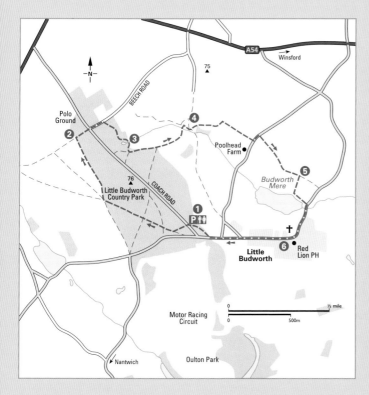

Distance 3.5 miles (5.7km)

Minimum Time 1hr 15min

Ascent/Gradient 98ft (30m) ▲▲▲

Level of Difficulty ●●●

Paths Easy tracks at first, field paths and some (usually quiet) road walking, 13 stiles

Landscape Mature woodland, open heath, farmland and mere

Suggested Map OS Explorer 267 Northwich & Delamere Forest

Start/Finish Grid reference: SJ 590654

Dog Friendliness Can run free in country park and fenced track

Parking Main car park for Little Budworth Country Park

Public Toilets At start

1 From the car park set off walking straight across the Coach Road to a path and then turn right on a wider path. Fork left and follow the main path, keeping straight on at a crossroads and carrying on again at the next crossing. When a field appears ahead, follow the path alongside to its right. This path veers away right, but you should go back left just before you reach a cleared area, by a Heathland Trail marker.

2 Go right on a wide track to the Coach Road and carry on straight across into Beech Road. After walking about 200yds (183m), turn right on a well-used path through open and very attractive woodland. Go through a gap in the fence, beyond which the path curves around a larger pool that is fringed with reeds and other vegetation – have a good look here, for this is a magnet for wildlife.

3 Cross a causeway/dam by the pool and gently climb a sunken track beyond. As it levels out, fork left by a Heathland Trail sign then turn left, with an open field not far away to the left. Bear left on a wider surfaced track, swinging down past houses to an ornamental pool in a dip. Immediately after this turn right on a sandy track.

4 Where another path crosses, most people evidently go through a gate ahead into the corner of the field. Strictly speaking, however, the right of way goes over a stile to its right then across the (very wet and smelly) corner of a wood to a second stile. From here bear right underneath a power line, carrying on as far as a stile in the far corner. Follow a narrow path (taking care to avoid nettles), then go over a stile on the right and straight across a large field. Aim just left of the farm to a gate and

stile. Go left on a lane for 60yds (55m) then right down a track. This becomes narrower, then descends slightly.

5 As the track levels out, there's a stile on the right, with a sign for Budworth Mere. Go down towards the water then left on a path skirting the mere. At the end go right up a road, swinging further right into the centre of Little Budworth.

6 Keep straight ahead along the road, going through the village then past open fields. Approaching the former entrance gates of Oulton Park, the pavement comes to an end. Here take a narrow woodland path on the right back to the car park.

45 The Dragon's Back

Climb the remains of an ancient coral reef

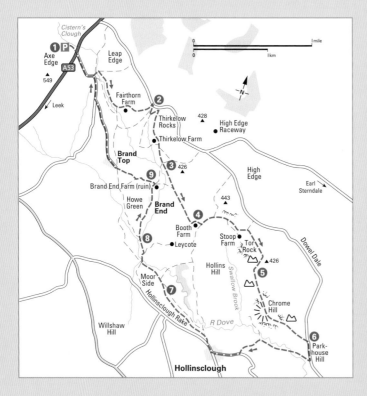

Distance 7.5 miles (12.1km)

Minimum Time 4hrs 30min

Ascent/Gradient 980ft (300m) ▲▲▲

Level of Difficulty ●●●

Paths Good paths except for ones between Hollinsclough and Brand End, can be slippery after rain, lots of stiles

Landscape Gritstone moors and cloughs with limestone hills

Suggested Map OS Explorer OL24 White Peak

Start/Finish Grid reference: SK 034697

Dog Friendliness Farmland, dogs should be kept under close control

Parking Axe Edge car park

Public Toilets None en route

1 From the car park cross the main road and descend the lane opposite. At the first right-hand bend turn left to take the left of two farm tracks, descending to cross the Cistern's Clough bridge heading for Fairthorn Farm. Past the house swing left on the drive up to the road at Thirkelow Rocks.

2 Turn right along the road for 200yds (183m), then take the farm track on the right, heading south past Thirkelow Farm. Take the right fork into the clough.

3 Where the track ends, veer slightly right to the waymarking posts highlighting a duckboard bridge and the route to Booth Farm.

4 Keep to the left of the farm and go over some steps in the wall ahead. After crossing a small field, turn left along the farm road, then fork right for Stoop Farm. Turn left along a waymarked field path, bypassing the farmhouse and climbing to a footpath intersection at the top wall. Take the path signposted 'Glutton Bridge via Chrome Hill'.

5 Drop down to a stile and follow a wallside path that eventually climbs left to the crest before continuing over the summit, and descending to the lane beneath the conical shape of Parkhouse Hill.

6 Turn right to walk along the lane, then right again to follow a farm track. Along the track, take the left fork to reach a surfaced road, which is just short of Hollinsclough. Walk through the village, going right at the junction, then cross over a stile on the right-hand side. Take the higher left fork that traverses Hollinsclough Rake.

7 On reaching the green zig-zag track at Moor Side, descend right to pass a ruin and continue up a narrow valley. Cross the stream and go over the stile to reach an old packhorse bridge. Across the bridge take a stony track up towards the farm buildings at Leycote. On a right-hand bend go left through a gate and follow a narrow path heading north-west into a wooded clough.

8 Follow the path across the simple slab bridge and up towards Brand End. Go right at the fork at the top. The path becomes a track, passing Brand End Cottage and descending to the ruins of Brand End Farm.

9 Turn left up the bank by a wall here, passing to the left of another farm. Turn left along a farm track to Brand Top. Here the road leads you back to Axe Edge.

46 The Goyt Valley of the Manchester Grimshawes

Admire the ruins of Errwood Hall and see the reservoir that caused the house's demolition

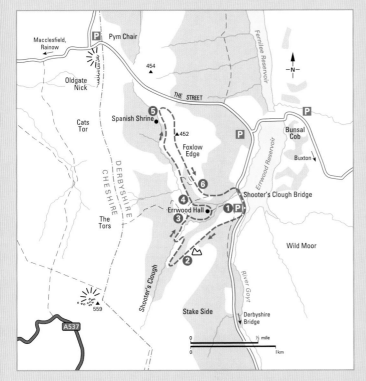

Distance 3.5 miles (5.7km)

Minimum Time 2hrs 30min

Ascent/Gradient 984ft (300m) ▲▲▲

Level of Difficulty ●●●

Paths Good paths and tracks, a few stiles

Landscape Park type woodland and moor

Suggested Map OS Explorer OL24 White Peak

Start/Finish Grid reference: SK 012748

Dog Friendliness Dogs should be kept under close control

Parking Errwood car park

Public Toilets 1 mile (1.6km) south at Derbyshire Bridge car park

1 The path, signposted 'Stakeside and the Cat and Fiddle', begins from the roadside south of the car park. Climb through a copse of trees, go straight across a cart track, then continue up the grassy spur that separates Shooter's Clough and the Goyt Valley.

2 Go through a gate in the wall (to the right) and follow a path that zig-zags through the woodland of Shooter's Clough before fording a stream. The path heads north (right), through rhododendron bushes before continuing across open grassland to a signposted junction of footpaths.

3 Turn right on a path skirting a wooded knoll, then ignore the first path through the gateposts and take the second left to Errwood Hall. Continue past the ruins, before descending steps to a footbridge.

4 Climb some steps on the right to reach another footpath signpost. Turn left along the path signposted 'Pym Chair'. This gradually swings north on hillslopes beneath Foxlow Edge. There's a short detour down and left to see the Spanish Shrine (which is visible from the main path).

5 About 100yds (91m) on from the Spanish Shrine, and before meeting the road at the very top, the path reaches open moorland. Take the narrow path forking right, which climbs to the top of Foxlow Edge. On reaching some old quarry workings near the top, the path is joined by a tumbledown dry-stone wall. Keep to the narrow corridor between the wall on the right and the fence on your left, ignoring little paths and tracks off to the right down into the valley. Continue the slow descent to the far end of the ridge.

6 At a fence corner, by the edge of woodland follow the path left, still downhill, around the edge of the trees and veer left again where it is joined by another path. With banks of rhododendrons on your right, follow the broad, gravelly track down through the woods to the roadside at Shooter's Clough Bridge. Turn right and cross the road bridge back to the car park.

47 Pennine Ways on Kinder Scout

Climb Jacob's Ladder to the viewpoint at Ringing Roger

Distance 7 miles (11.3km)

Minimum Time 4hrs

Ascent/Gradient 1,650ft (500m) ▲▲▲

Level of Difficulty ●●●

Paths Rock and peat paths, some steep ascents and descents

Landscape Heather moor

Suggested Map OS Explorer OL1 Dark Peak

Start/Finish Grid reference: SK 125853

Dog Friendliness Walk is on farmland and access agreement land. Dogs should be kept on leads

Parking Edale pay car park

Public Toilets At car park

1 Turn right out of the car park and head north into Edale (the village), under the railway and past The Old Nags Head pub. By a gate at the far end turn right and then follow the path across the footbridge that leads over Grinds Brook.

2 Leave the main Grindsbrook Clough path by the side of a small barn, taking the right fork that climbs up the lower hill slope to reach a stile on the edge of open country. Beyond the stile the path zig-zags above Fred Heardman's Plantation then climbs up the nose of The Nab to the skyline rocks. Where the path divides, take the rather eroded right fork to the summit of Ringing Roger.

3 Pause to enjoy the views then follow the edge path left, rounding the cavernous hollow of Grindsbrook past Nether Tor. The walk meets the old Pennine Way route on the east side, at a place marked by a large cairn.

4 Ignoring the left fork to the outlier of Grindslow Knoll, follow the paved footpath westwards to the head of another deep hollow, the clough of Crowden Brook.

5 Cross Crowden Brook, then leave the edge to follow a narrow, level path traversing slopes on the left beneath the outcrop of Crowden Tower. Below the tower, turn left for a steep, bumpy track down the grassy hillside to the brook. Keep to the path that follows the brook, fording it on several occasions.

6 Go over a stile at the edge of open country, then cross a footbridge shaded by tall rowans to change to the west bank. From here the path threads through woodland before descending in steps to the road at Upper Booth. You now need to follow the Pennine Way path back to Edale.

7 Turn left along the road and left again into the farmyard of Upper Booth Farm before exiting at the top right corner. After following a track to a gateway, bear left uphill to a stile by an old barn. Here the Way traverses fields at the foot of Broadlee Bank before joining a tree-lined track into the village. Turn right along the road back to the car park.

48 Around Eastwood in the Steps of D. H. Lawrence

Explore the countryside around the Nottinghamshire town that provided inspiration for much of the writer's work

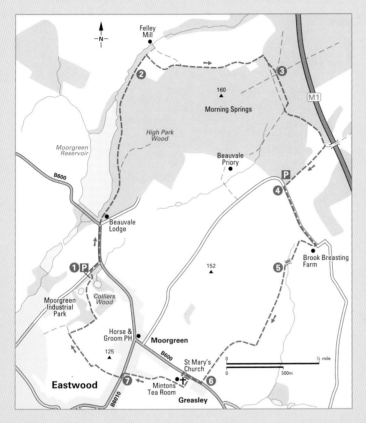

Distance 5.75 miles (9.2km)

Minimum Time 2hrs 30min

Ascent/Gradient 360ft (110m) ▲▲▲

Level of Difficulty ●●●

Paths Rough field and woodland tracks, 2 stiles

Landscape Farmland and woods, red-brick towns and villages

Suggested Map OS Explorer 260 Nottingham

Start/Finish Grid reference: SK 481481

Dog Friendliness On lead at start (poop scoop by-laws apply)

Parking Colliers Wood car park, Engine Lane, off B600

Public Toilets None en route (nearest in Eastwood)

1 Walk out of the entrance of Colliers Wood car park and turn right, then left along the pavement of the B600. At the bend turn right by Beauvale Lodge and take the track to its left (signposted 'Felley Mill'). Walk through High Park Wood, above Moorgreen Reservoir, branching left after 0.25 mile (400m) just before a gate. Carry on along the main track until an open field appears on your right.

2 Continue walking for 150yds (137m), then turn right at the stile and walk up the left-hand side of a line of trees separating two fields. At the far side turn left, follow the woodland edge, go around the corner and continue alongside the forest. After 0.5 mile (800m) turn right beyond the bench to locate a public footpath through the trees.

3 Where the public footpath emerges at a junction of three forest rides go straight ahead. With the growl of the nearby M1 motorway getting louder, turn left after the bend on to a clearly indicated footpath into the woods. This emerges to follow the edge of a field, swinging right on the far side and eventually reaching a lay-by.

4 Turn right if you want to view the remains of Beauvale Priory, otherwise go left and walk down the lane to the bend by the intriguingly named Brook Breasting Farm. Go sharply right, following along the left-hand edge of a field, then turn left and drop down through two more fields. Look for the gap in the undergrowth on the right-hand side, and go over a footbridge.

5 Turn left and follow the sign across the lower field. Continue along the top edge of successive fields, going right to skirt the final sloping field, then drop down to the road.

6 Cross over and turn right to enter the churchyard of St Mary's at Greasley. Walk around the church and exit the churchyard at the far side on a footpath signposted 'Moorgreen'. After crossing the cemetery, go across the field and continue to walk alongside paddocks to reach the road at the top.

7 Turn left and then right for a path between houses. Follow waymarks across and down through fields, and at the bottom go right for the path back into Colliers Wood. Turn first left to reach the ponds, and beyond is the car park.

49 A Merrie Tale of Sherwood Forest

Walk where outlaw Robin Hood reputedly robbed the rich

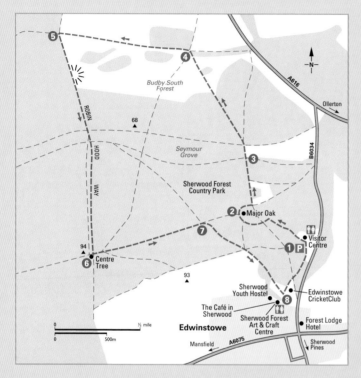

Distance 5.5 miles (8.8km)

Minimum Time 2hrs 30min

Ascent/Gradient 278ft (85m) ▲▲▲

Level of Difficulty ●●●

Paths Easy woodland tracks and wide forest rides

Landscape Beautiful mixed woodland, more open to north

Suggested Map OS Explorer 270 Sherwood Forest

Start/Finish Grid reference: SK 626676

Dog Friendliness On lead around Visitor Centre, otherwise excellent

Parking Sherwood Forest visitor centre (pay-and-display)

Public Toilets Sherwood Forest Visitor Centre

1 Facing the main entrance to Sherwood Forest visitor centre from the car park, turn left and follow the well-signposted route 'the Major Oak'.

2 Go along the curving path as it completes a semi-circle around the impressive old tree and continue as far as the junction with a public bridleway (signposted). Turn left here, then walk this straight and uncomplicated route for around 0.25 mile (400m), ignoring all paths that lead off.

3 At a green notice board, which gives warning of a nearby military training area, the main path bears left. Ignoring this, go straight ahead, past the metal bar gate, for a path that continues over a crossroads to become a wide, fenced track through pleasant open country of heather and bracken known as Budby South Forest.

4 At the very far side go through a gate and turn left on to an unmade lane, and walk this undulating route for 0.75 mile (1.2km).

5 At the major junction just before the plantation begins, turn left, indicated 'Centre Tree'. With the rows of conifers on your right, and good views across Budby South Forest on your left, keep to this straight track. Where the track divides into two parallel trails, the gravelly track on the right is the cycle route, while the more leafy and grassy ride to the left is the bridleway, but either can be used.

6 When you reach the Centre Tree — a huge spreading oak — the two routes converge to continue past a bench down a wide avenue among the trees. Don't go down this, but instead turn left and, ignoring paths off right and left, carry straight on along the main track back into the heart of the forest.

7 After almost 0.75 mile (1.2km) you pass a metal bar gate on the right and then meet a bridleway coming in from the left. Ignoring the inviting path straight ahead (which returns to the Major Oak) bear right on the main track, past some bare holes and dips hollowed out by children's bikes. At a large junction of criss-crossing routes go straight on (signposted 'Fairground') so that an open field and distant housing becomes visible to your right. This wide sandy track descends to a field by Edwinstowe cricket ground. The Art and Craft Centre and Sherwood Youth Hostel are on the far side, and the village centre beyond.

8 To return to the visitor centre and car park, follow the well-walked, signposted track back up past the cricket ground.

50 Churches of the Wolds

Explore two beautiful Lincolnshire villages through their contrasting churches

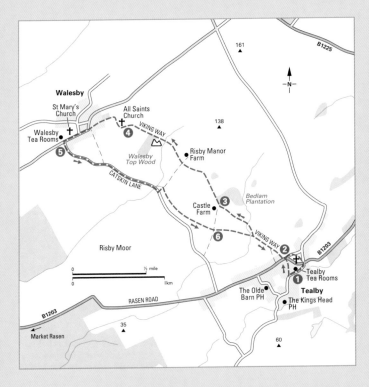

Distance 4.25 miles (6.8km)

Minimum Time 2hrs

Ascent/Gradient 721ft (220m) ▲▲▲

Level of Difficulty ●●●

Paths Field paths, some steep and others muddy

Landscape Undulating chalk hills, deep valleys and woodland

Suggested Map OS Explorer 282 Lincolnshire Wolds North

Start/Finish Grid reference: TF 157907

Dog Friendliness On lead near livestock, fine on hedged tracks and lanes

Parking Front Street, Tealby, near tea rooms

Public Toilets None en route (nearest in Market Rasen)

1 From the Tealby Tea Rooms walk down Front Street as far as B Leaning & Sons, a butcher and maker of traditional Lincolnshire sausages established in 1860. Turn right into Church Lane, which soon becomes a walkway. At the top, turn left and cross over Rasen Road to follow the public footpath that runs between houses on the opposite side. As far as Walesby you will be following the Norse helmet waymarks of the Viking Way.

2 Pass through a gate and cross open pasture, aiming for another gate in the far bottom corner. Go through this and along the path ahead, ignoring a footbridge to the left. Walk up the open hillside ahead to reach the corner of Bedlam Plantation which is above Castle Farm.

3 Turn right and go through a gate for a fenced path beside the woods. At the far end head diagonally left down a grassy field to pass below Risby Manor Farm. Cross the lane leading up to the farmhouse and continue ahead, crossing a deep valley and climbing steeply towards Walesby Top Wood. Pass through a gate and keep straight ahead across a field of crops to reach All Saints Church.

4 Walk through the churchyard and continue along the Viking Way as it drops down a wide track into the village. When you reach Rasen Road at the bottom go straight on, past the 'new' parish church of St Mary until you reach the junction with Catskin Lane.

5 If you need refreshment, cross the road to visit Walesby Tea Rooms. Otherwise turn left and walk along Catskin Lane for 0.75 mile (1.2km). Just past a right-hand curve,

turn left at the entrance of a farm drive and go over a cattle grid. This is in fact a public bridleway that leads back up to the hilltop, but you should turn right in a few paces and join a footpath across rough pasture, initially parallel with the road. Stay on this path as it runs along the left-hand side of a field to arrive at the drive to Castle Farm.

6 The public footpath now continues almost due east across the vast sloping field beyond. When you reach the far side of the field, pass through a gate and drop down to cross a wooden footbridge. Turn right on the far side of the bridge to rejoin the earlier route back into Tealby, this time turning left up Rasen Road to visit All Saints Church. Drop down through the churchyard and follow Beck Hill to the memorial hall, then turn right along Front Street to return to the start of the walk.

51 It All Comes Out in the Wilds of The Wash

Explore sea walls and tidal mudflats on the South Lincolnshire coast

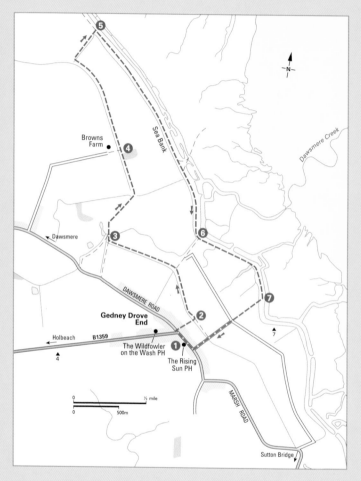

Distance 5.75 miles (9.2km)

Minimum Time 2hrs 30min

Ascent/Gradient Negligible ▲ ▲ ▲

Level of Difficulty ● ● ●

Paths Field, 1 stile

Landscape Open arable fields and bare marsh and mudflats

Suggested Map OS Explorer 249 Spalding & Holbeach

Start/Finish Grid reference: TF 463292

Dog Friendliness Overhead military planes on weekdays can be very loud

Parking Roadside parking in centre of Gedney Drove End (off A17 east of Holbeach)

Public Toilets None en route

1 With your back to The Rising Sun pub, turn left and walk along Dawsmere Road past the junction and take the signposted public footpath on the right, between bungalows. At the far side of the field go across a small footbridge and up some steps in order to turn left into a wide field.

2 For 1 mile (1.6km) walk along the edge of this field, which is in fact the line of the former sea wall, keeping more or less parallel with the present and much higher sea bank over to your right. As a sign indicates, continue straight ahead at the point where the old sea bank veers invitingly away to the right.

3 When the field ends turn right for 50yds (46m) then, faced with a small thicket, drop down to the farm track on your left. Turn right, and follow the main route (ignore the lower track) alongside a narrow shelter-belt of woodland. This wide, gravel track heads out towards the sea bank then bends left and continues past Browns Farm.

4 Stay on the main track for about 0.75 mile (1.2km) beyond the farm, then go right by an old wartime pill box for a short path over to the sea wall.

5 Turn right and follow either the grassy top of the sea bank (a public right of way) or the surfaced lane just below it past a succession of military observation towers. The bombing range is spread out before you, with the low Norfolk coast over to your right and the Lincolnshire seaboard towards Boston and Skegness leftwards.

6 After the third tower ignore the gated road that heads off inland (a short cut back to Gedney), but instead continue along the sea bank past one final watchtower until you reach a stile. Cross the stile and continue ahead for another 400yds (366m).

7 Turn right at a public footpath sign, down some steps, for a direct path along a field-edge to the junction of an open lane. Here continue straight ahead into Gedney, turning right at the end back on to Dawsmere Road.

55 Fairburn Ings and Ledsham

Cross a bird reserve of national importance and visit the picturesque village of Ledsham

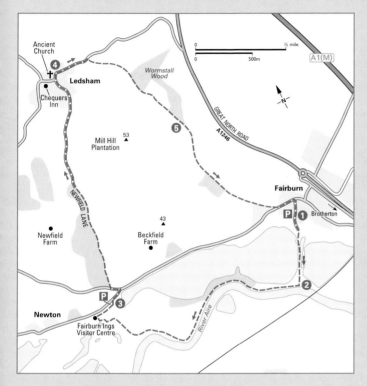

Distance 5 miles (8km)

Minimum Time 2hrs 30min

Ascent/Gradient 262ft (80m) ▲▲▲

Level of Difficulty ●●●

Paths Good paths and tracks, 2 stiles

Landscape Lakes, riverside and reclaimed colliery spoil heaps

Suggested Map OS Explorer 289 Leeds

Start/Finish Grid reference: SE 470278

Dog Friendliness Keep on lead around main lake, due to wildfowl

Parking Free parking in Cut Road, Fairburn, 100yds (91m) west of the Three Horseshoes pub, in the direction of Fairburn Ings

Public Toilets Fairburn Ings visitor centre

1 Walk down Cut Road as it narrows to a track. Soon you have the main lake to your right, and a smaller stretch of water to your left, overlooked by a hide, which is reached via a short detour. The ongoing route, however, follows the main path ahead and leads to a junction by the River Aire.

2 Go right through a kissing gate along the top of a wooded ridge (actually an old spoil heap), with the river to your left and the lake right. Look out for a couple of other bird hides, before you lose sight of the lake. The path crosses a broader expanse of spoil heap through open scrub, following the river before curving right above another small mere. At the bottom, swing left into more trees and then,

opposite a sculpted frog, go right on a wooden walkway across a marsh to the visitor centre. Leave through the car park to a lane.

3 Go right for 100yds (91m), then go left (signed 'Ledston and Kippax') for just 100yds (91m), and pick up a path on your right that hugs the right-hand fringe of a wood. Beyond the wood, take a path between fields; it broadens to a track as you approach the village of Ledsham. At an estate of houses, turn right, along Manor Garth.

4 You arrive in the village by the ancient church. Walk right, along the road (or, for refreshments, go left to Chequers Inn). Beyond the village, where the road bears left, leave

ahead through a gate on the bend on to an undulating track. Over a stile, walk towards woodland and continue within its periphery. Leave the wood by a stile and carry on along the foot of a rising pasture. Another stile at the far bottom corner takes the way through a narrow spur of woodland.

5 Head slightly left, uphill, across the next field, to follow a fence and hedgerow bounding the top. Keep ahead through kissing gates, remaining at the field-edge and passing barns that stand over to the left. Through a final gate, a developing track leads downhill. Go left, when you meet the road, and back into the village of Fairburn to get back to the start of the walk.

56 Beautiful Hurst Green and the Three Rivers

Investigate Lancashire fields and river banks familiar to Tolkien, who often stayed locally

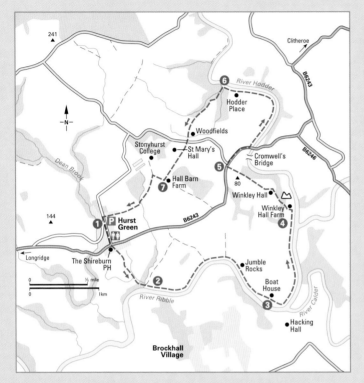

Distance 6.5 miles (10.4km)

Minimum Time 2hrs

Ascent/Gradient 459ft (140m) ▲▲▲

Level of Difficulty ●●●

Paths Grassy riverside paths, woodland and farm tracks, 11 stiles

Landscape Pastoral scenery, scattered woodlands, backdrop of moors

Suggested Map OS Explorer 287 West Pennine Moors

Start/Finish Grid reference: SD 684382

Dog Friendliness Can run free in woodland sections

Parking By Hurst Green village hall or on roadside adjacent

Public toilets Centre of Hurst Green

1 Walk down the road to reach the centre of Hurst Green village. Cross the main road and go down to the left of The Shireburn pub to a stile below the main car park. Go down the edge of a field and then follow a small stream to reach some duckboards and a footbridge. After a slight rise, descend via a stile and winding path to the River Ribble. Bear left just above the river.

2 Skirt the aqueduct and return to the river bank. Join a surfaced drive past Jumbles Rocks. Go over a large wooden stile beyond a small stone building to rejoin the river bank and follow it, towards the Boat House.

3 After rounding the big bend, go up slightly to a track. Follow this for about 0.5 mile (800m). Opposite the confluence of the Ribble and the Hodder, go over a stile by a bench.

4 The narrow path quickly rejoins the track. At Winkley Hall Farm go left to the houses, right between barns then left past a pond and out into a lane. This climbs steeply then levels out, swinging left past Winkley Hall. Go through a kissing gate on the right and across the field to another. Keep straight on across a large field, just left of a wood, then down via a stile and up to reach a road.

5 Turn right along a pavement to the river. Immediately before the bridge, turn left along a track. Follow the river round, then climb up past Hodder Place before descending again to a bridge over a stream.

6 Go up the track on the left, cross a footbridge and then climb a long flight of wooden steps. Follow the top edge of a plantation, then cross a stile into a field. Keep

to its edge and at the end cross a stile into a stony track. Keep left, past Woodfields and out to the road. Go down the track by the post-box to Hall Barn Farm and along the right side of the buildings.

7 Turn right and walk along a tarmac track for 200yds (183m). Go left through a gate by the end of a wall and along a narrow field. Drop down to the right on a track alongside a wood then up to a kissing gate. Follow the field-edge to another kissing gate. At the top of the final field, through a gate, a narrow path leads to a short lane. At its end turn left back to the start of the walk.

57 Hidden York

Make your way along the cobbled lanes and medieval thoroughfares of an ancient city

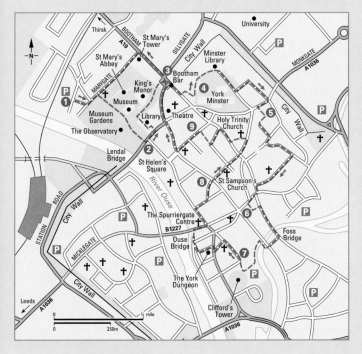

Distance 3.25 miles (5.3km)

Minimum Time 1hr 30min

Ascent/Gradient 82ft (25m) ▲▲▲

Level of Difficulty ●●●

Paths City pavements

Landscape Historic city

Suggested Map AA Street by Street York (page 2 C3)

Start/Finish Grid reference: SE 598523

Dog Friendliness City streets, so dogs should be kept on a lead

Parking Marygate Car Park, off Bootham

Public Toilets Museum Gardens and Bootham Bar

1 Walk back into Marygate, turn left, cross the road and enter Museum Gardens through the archway. Follow the path straight ahead, passing the Observatory, and leave the gardens by the lodge.

2 Turn left, then left again towards the library. Go left through a gate, and along the side of the library. Go up the steps, and through a gate in the wall. At the bottom of the slope, turn right and follow Abbey Wall into Exhibition Square.

3 Cross at the traffic-lights and go through Bootham Bar. A few paces on your left, take a passageway beside The Hole in the Wall pub and turn right down Precentor's Court. By the Minster, go left through the gate, signed 'York Minster Dean's Park'.

4 Follow the path left to the Minster Library building. Bend right through the gate and along the cobbled road. Turn left by the

postbox down Chapter House Street, bending right into Ogleforth. At the crossroads turn right, then go left through an archway opposite The National Trust Café.

5 Bear right into Bartle Garth, which bends left. At the T-junction turn right, and then go left down Spen Lane. Opposite Hilary House, go right along St Saviourgate. At the T-junction turn left, then right at the crossroads. Next to Jones's shoe shop on the left, take a passage, Lady Peckitt's Yard.

6 Go under the buildings, then turn left to Fossgate. Turn right, go over the bridge and then turn right along Merchantgate. At the T-junction, cross the road and take the glazed walkway beside the bridge, signed 'Castle Area', into the car park by Clifford's Tower.

7 Bend right and go to the right of the Hilton Hotel. Just after passing the church on the right, go left down Friargate, right

along Clifford Street, and then left by The York Dungeon. At the riverside turn right, ascend the steps by Ouse Bridge and turn right again. At the traffic-lights, turn left by The Spurriergate Centre. By the NatWest Bank go right, forking left into Feasegate.

8 Go ahead to cross Parliament Street and pass St Sampson's Church. Go straight on at the next crossroads into Goodramgate. After 50yds (46m), go left through a gateway into Holy Trinity churchyard, and leave by a passage to the left of the tower, to reach Low Petergate. Turn right, then take the next left into Grape Lane. Where it bends left, turn right down the narrow Coffee Yard into Stonegate.

9 Go left to St Helen's Square and turn right by Lloyds TSB. Go straight on at the next crossroads back to Exhibition Square. At the traffic-lights, turn left up Bootham. Turn left down Marygate by the circular tower to return to the car park.

58 Down to the Summit on Clougha Pike

Get a close look at several 'cloughs' or channels cut at the end of the last ice age

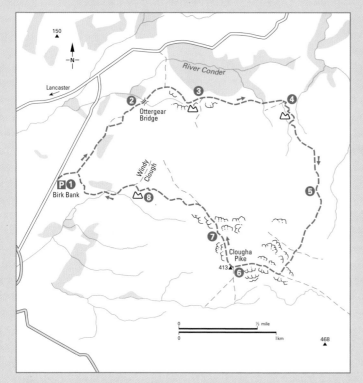

Distance 5.25 miles (8.4km)

Minimum Time 2hrs

Ascent/Gradient 1,050ft (320m) ▲▲▲

Level of Difficulty ●●●

Paths Mostly very rough moorland, often rocky, 4 stiles

Landscape Moorland with some rocky outcrops, above green valley

Suggested Map OS Explorer OL41 Forest of Bowland & Ribblesdale

Start/Finish Grid reference: SD 526604

Dog Friendliness Access Area – dogs not permitted

Parking Access Area car park at Birk Bank

Public Toilets Nearest at Crook O'Lune

1 Follow the track above the car park, then fork left. It becomes a green path, running generally level, to Ottergear Bridge.

2 Turn left and walk along a level track, then bear right at the next junction. The track climbs slightly, descends into a narrow valley, then climbs steeply up the far side before it finally eases and swings round to the right.

3 Go left on a narrow path, running almost level above a steeper slope. After 500yds (457m), it angles back down into the valley. Follow the base of the steep slope and cross a small stream. After 30yds (27m) a green track climbs to the right.

4 Wind up steeply to near-level moor. The path follows a slight groove, then skirts leftward around a boggy patch parallel to the

wall. The grassy path ahead is initially very faint. Keep just left of the continuous heather and it soon becomes clearer. There's another grooved section, then a clear stony path rises leftward across steeper ground.

5 As the slope eases the path remains clear, passing a few sketchy cairns. Follow a groove, past tumbledown shooting butts. As the ground levels, ease right past cairns and marker stakes to a new track. Cross and follow a thin grassy path with more marker stakes. Bear right up a slight rise and join a wider path at a cairn. Go right on a broad ridge, crossing a fence, to reach the summit trig point.

6 Descend a clear path on the right past a large cairn. There's a steep drop nearby on the left, with some small crags. A fence converges from the right, meeting a wall.

7 Scramble down rocks by the end of the wall. Continue down its left side for about 300yds (274m). Bear left at a levelling amid scattered boulders. Descend through a gap flanked by wrinkled rocks then across gentler slopes to a gate by the corner of a wall.

8 Head straight down until the ground steepens, then swing right and weave down towards Windy Clough. From a stile go left down a grooved path to an area of young trees. Fork left, closer to the stream, rejoining wetter alternative routes above larger oaks. Descend through gorse then follow duckboards skirting a bog. Turn right along a track then left over a slight rise to the car park.

59 A Kingdom for a Horse

Take a walk fit for a king – and admire some thoroughbreds

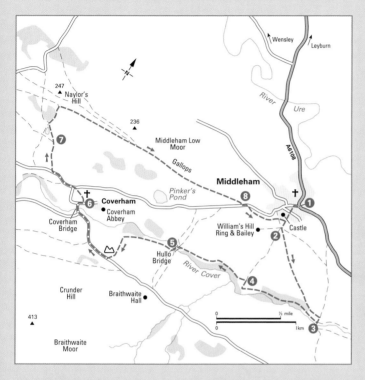

Distance 7 miles (11.3km)

Minimum Time 2hrs 30min

Ascent/Gradient 475ft (145m) ▲▲▲

Level of Difficulty ●●●

Paths Field paths and tracks, with some road walking, 14 stiles

Landscape Gentle farmland, riverside paths, views of Wensleydale

Suggested Map OS Explorer OL 30 Yorkshire Dales – Northern & Central

Start/Finish Grid reference: SE 127877

Dog Friendliness Livestock and horses in fields, so dogs on leads

Parking In square in centre of Middleham

Public Toilets Middleham

1 From the square, take the Coverham road then turn left up a passageway beside the Castle Keep Tea Rooms. Continue to the left of Middleham Castle, along a walled track towards a gate.

2 Bear left across the big field, following the sign for 'stepping stones'. Cross two more fields, clambering over waymarked stiles. After the third stile, follow the field-edge above a steep bank. When you reach a a crossing wall turn right, going down to the River Cover by the stepping stones.

3 Turn right (do not cross the river) and follow the path along through woods and a field. A gate leads to some steps and an elevated section. After returning to the river bank, cross a stile into a field. After another stile at its end, turn immediately right. Climb steeply to a marker post.

4 Turn left and follow the edge of a wood. At the end of the field, go left through the trees, then straight ahead on an obvious descending path. Cross a stile and turn left to Hullo Bridge.

5 Cross the bridge and turn right on a permissive path, crossing three stiles. At a crossing wire fence turn left. Cross another stile. Where the fence bends right, go ahead up a steep bank to reach a gate on to a lane. Turn right and descend to Coverham Bridge. Cross the bridge and turn right on a track.

6 Before iron gates, turn left through a small gate, climbing beside a waterfall into the churchyard. Leave by the lychgate and bear left along the main road (signed 'Forbidden Corner'). After 0.25 mile (400m), go through a gate on the right opposite a disused factory. Bear slightly left, cross three stiles, then aim

for a prominent gap between buildings and continue through a narrow strip of woodland.

7 Bear slightly left to a stile, to the right of a stone wall. Skirt ornamental ponds to meet a track. Turn right and then ascend, past a house, to a gateway on to a wider track. Turn right. Where the track bends right, keep straight ahead across the grassy moor; look for occasional blue-topped posts marking the line of a bridleway. When the long fenced gallops appear, keep them to your left and continue down to the road.

8 Turn left. Just before the Middleham sign, take a signposted path on the right. Cross the stile, turn left and follow the path parallel to the road. Go through a stile and a gate, then bear left down to another stile and go through a gate on to the lane. Turn left and make your way back to the square.

60 Herriot's Darrowby

Follow in the footsteps of James Herriot through town and country

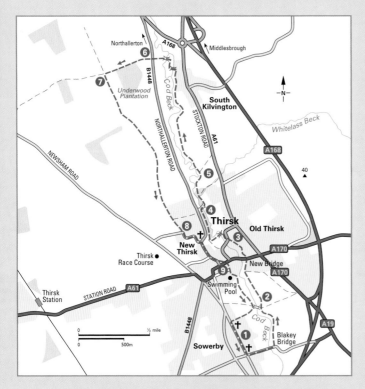

Distance 5 miles (8km)

Minimum Time 2hrs

Ascent/Gradient 66ft (20m) ▲▲▲

Level of Difficulty ●●●

Paths Town paths, field paths and tracks, 6 stiles

Landscape Streamside and undulating pastureland around town

Suggested Map OS Explorer 302 Northallerton & Thirsk

Start/Finish Grid reference: SE 430813

Dog Friendliness Keep dogs on leads

Parking Roadside parking in the main street of Sowerby village

Public Toilets Thirsk town centre

1 Walk down the village street, away from Thirsk. Just past the Methodist Church on the left, go left down Blakey Lane. Cross the bridge, turn left on a signed path and follow the stream, going through two kissing gates to a footbridge.

2 Continue beside the stream to a stile. Go through two gates to a car park and ahead to the road. Cross and take a path that curves left, then right by the bridge. At a paved area, turn right to go alongside a green to a road.

3 Cross the road and continue straight ahead, crossing a main road and going left at the top of the green. Cross the metal bridge and continue beside the beck by the church. Before reaching the road take the path heading to the right, beside a bench, to a footbridge on the right.

4 Cross the bridge and go straight ahead through two gates, curving left to follow the beck to a gate by a bridge. Go straight ahead (not over the bridge) and follow the path across the fields, veering diagonally right to a stile on your right.

5 Climb over the stile and then follow the stream, going over another two stiles as you pass beside houses. Continue left over a footbridge by some mill buildings. At this point the path winds right in order to cross a second footbridge. Follow the bridleway sign across the field and then through a gate to reach the main road.

6 Cross the road and go through a signed gate opposite, to another gate beside a wood. 150yds (137m) after the wood, turn left at a waymark.

7 Walk down the field with a hedge on your left. In the second field, go left over a stile and continue with the hedge on your right, bearing half left to another stile. Continue across the field, then down the next field-edge, bearing left, then right at the end to a path that becomes a grassy lane between hedges.

8 At a road go straight ahead, bearing left, then right past the church. Turn right into the town centre. In the Market Place, cross towards the Golden Fleece. Go down a signed passageway two premises to the pub's left, cross a lane and go down Villa Place.

9 Bear left to pass the swimming pool. Turn right round the pool building to a gate. Go ahead and parallel with the beck. At the bridge, turn right on a grassy track to a gate on to a lane, then straight to Sowerby.

61 Roseberry Topping and Captain Cook Country

Pay your respects to Captain James Cook and walk through beautiful flower-carpeted woodland

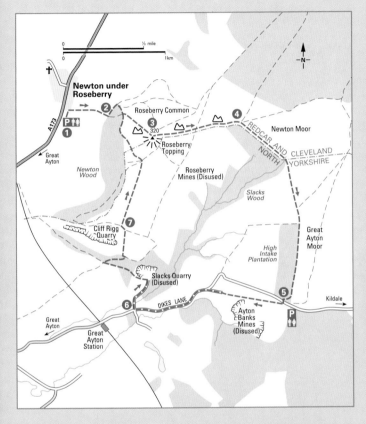

Distance 5.5 miles (8.8km)

Minimum Time 2hrs 30min

Ascent/Gradient 1,214ft (370m) ▲▲▲

Level of Difficulty ●●●

Paths Hillside climb, then tracks and field paths, 5 stiles

Landscape One of the best 360-degree views in Yorkshire

Suggested Map OS Explorer OL 26 North York Moors – Western

Start/Finish Grid reference: NZ 570128

Dog Friendliness Off lead, except in farmland

Parking Car park on A173 just south of Newton under Roseberry

Public Toilets In car park at foot of Roseberry Topping

1 Take the rough lane beside the car park towards Roseberry Topping. The path goes through a gateway then rises to a second gate at the beginning of the woodland.

2 Go through the gate into National Trust Land and then turn left. There is a well-worn, mostly paved path to the summit. It is a stiff climb to the trig point on the top of the hill.

3 From the summit, walk east from the trig point, past two iron poles set into rock, and straight on along the paved way. Go steeply downhill. At the bottom, bear right to go up a track that bends right around the corner of woodland to a gate.

4 Go through the gate and take the path alongside the wood, following yellow waymarkers. Continue on the path until it eventually follows a wall and descends the hillside to reach a road.

5 Turn right, cross the cattle grid and bear left between two benches, then go right, along the fence line, at first parallel with the road. Go down the field, through a gate and then over a stile and out into a lane. Walk past the cottages to reach a road, where you go straight ahead.

6 At a crossroads go right, down Aireyholme Lane. Follow the lane as it winds past houses, then take a signed footpath left over

a stile. Follow the fence to two gates into woodland. After 0.5 mile (800m), go right at a National Trust sign, up a path ascending through the woods to a signposted stile. Over it, turn left to another stile, then after it, go right along the edge of the woodland. Bend left to a gate near a house.

7 Walk across two fields to a stile, then continue uphill to the tower. Beyond it, take a grassy path left down a gully, to a gate into woodland. Follow the path downhill through the woods to return to the gate at the top of the lane leading back to the car park.

62 From Eskdale to Miterdale

Discover gentle hills that were once a royal hunting forest

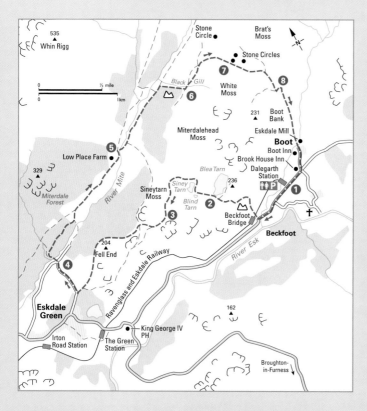

Distance 6.75 miles (10.9km)

Minimum Time 4hrs

Ascent/Gradient 1,312ft (400m) ▲▲▲

Level of Difficulty ●●●

Paths Good paths in valleys, but often indistinct on hills, 4 stiles

Landscape Heath and moor with views across surrounding valleys

Suggested Map OS Explorer OL6 The English Lakes (SW)

Start/Finish Grid reference: NY 173007

Dog Friendliness Keep on lead as sheep roam moors

Parking Car park beside Dalegarth Station (pay-and-display)

Public Toilets At Dalegarth Station

Note Walk not advised in poor visibility

1 Follow the lane down the valley towards Beckfoot Bridge. Before the railway halt, cross the line to a gate where a zig-zag path to Blea Tarn is signed up the hillside. Approaching the tarn, go left crossing a stream.

2 A vague path maintains the firm ground, right of Blind and Siney tarns, then, at a fork, bear left. Beyond a lone tree, go left again. The way is marshy around Sineytarn Moss but a dry route can be found. Eventually, the route joins a wall, dropping to level grass.

3 Bear right to a fence stile by a forest and continue along its edge below Fell End. Keep going near the wall, reaching its corner in about 0.75 mile (1.2km). A short track on the right descends to a junction, and another right turn takes you into Miterdale.

4 Emerge on to a tarmac lane at the bottom and go through a gate opposite into Miterdale Forest. Drop over the river and then bear right on an undulating, weaving path above its far bank. A lateral wall shortly forces you uphill on to a forest track. Turn right and follow the track out of the trees, joining another track from the right to continue up the valley to Low Place Farm.

5 Walk past the farmhouse and through a second yard, leaving by the right-hand gates, signed 'Wasdale'. Follow the river upstream before crossing a bridge to a track that continues along its opposite bank. Keep ahead for nearly 0.75 mile (1.2km) until you cross a stile at the far end of a plantation. Here, leave the track and climb the hill beside the trees to another stile at the top.

6 Bear left above Black Gill and then continue parallel to a wall towards the higher ground of Low Longrigg. After 400yds (366m) strike right on a barely visible path, making for the stone circles, which briefly break the horizon.

7 Bear right at the second circle and, after passing beneath a rocky outcrop, fork left. The way is still vague, but now drops towards stone huts, where a clear path descends by them to the right.

8 Follow it down Boot Bank and into Boot, and cross Whillan Beck by Eskdale Mill to continue through the village. At the end turn right to Dalegarth Station.

63 Brant Fell Above Bowness-on-Windermere

Escape the crowds to find peace and solitude on the hills above Bowness

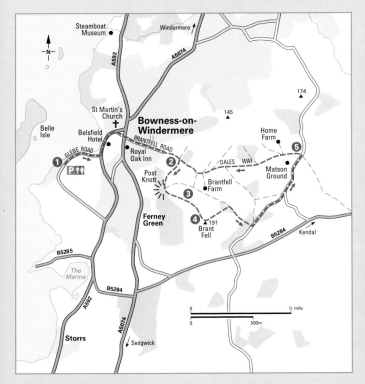

Distance 3.5 miles (5.7km)

Minimum Time 1hr 15min

Ascent/Gradient 525ft (160m) ▲▲▲

Level of Difficulty ●●●

Paths Pavement, road, stony tracks, grassy paths, 2 stiles

Landscape Town, mixed woodland, open fell, lake and fell views

Suggested Map OS Explorer OL7 The English Lakes (SE)

Start/Finish Grid reference: SD 398966

Dog Friendliness Popular route for dogs; busy roads and sheep grazing, so must be under control

Parking Fee car park on Glebe Road above Windermere lake

Public Toilets At car park and above information centre

1 Take Glebe Road into Bowness town. Swing left and, opposite the steamer pier, go right over the main Windermere road and then turn left. Opposite the impressive Church of St Martin turn right to ascend the little street of St Martins Hill. Cross the Kendal road to climb Brantfell Road directly above. At the head of the road a little iron gate leads on to the Dales Way, a grassy and stony path that climbs directly up the hillside. Continue to a kissing gate by the wood, leading on to a lane.

2 Pass through the kissing gate and turn right, signposted 'Post Knott', to follow the stony lane. Continue on the lane rising through the woods until it crests a height near the flat circular top of Post Knott. Bear left and make the short ascent to the summit. The view from here was once exceptional but is now obscured by trees. Retrace a few steps back to the track

then bear right to find a kissing gate leading out of the wood on to the open hillside.

3 Beyond the kissing gate take the grassy path, rising to a rocky shoulder. Cross the shoulder and first descend, then ascend to a ladder stile in the top corner of the field by some fir trees. Cross the stile then bear right to ascend directly up the open, grassy flanks of Brant Fell to its rocky summit.

4 Go left (northeast) from the top of the fell, following a line of cairns down to a kissing gate. Descend through a young plantation to a second gate and a track. Turn right and follow the track to a stile and gate leading out to a road. Turn left along the road and continue left at the junction, to pass Matson Ground. Immediately beyond is a kissing gate on the left, waymarked for the Dales Way.

5 Go through the kissing gate and continue down the path to cross a track and pass through a kissing gate into another field. Keep along the track beneath the trees and beside a new pond, until the path swings left to emerge through a kissing gate on to a surfaced drive. Go right along the drive for 30yds (27m) until the path veers off left through the trees to follow the fence. An iron gate leads into a field. Follow the grassy path, first descending and then rising to an iron gate in the corner of the field. Continue to join a grassy track and go through the kissing gate. Cross the surfaced drive of Brantfell Farm and keep straight on to another kissing gate leading into a field. Follow the path, parallel to the wall, descending the hill to intercept a track, via a kissing gate, and regain Point 2. Retrace your steps back to Glebe Road and return back to the car park.

64 Around Lake Buttermere

Experience the Lake District's only lakeside tunnel as you hug the shore of Buttermere

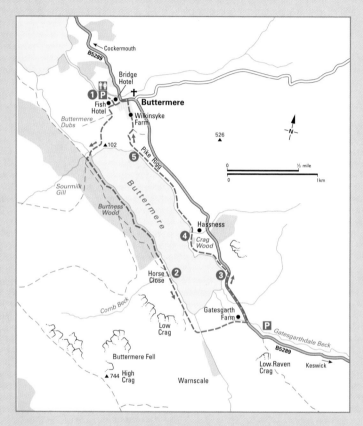

Distance 4.5 miles (7.2km)

Minimum Time 2hrs

Ascent/Gradient 35ft (11m) ▲▲▲

Level of Difficulty ●●●

Paths Good path, some road walking, 2 stiles

Landscape Lake, fells, woodland and farmland

Suggested Map OS Explorer OL4 The English Lakes (NW)

Start/Finish Grid reference: NY 173169

Dog Friendliness On leads near farms and open fells where sheep are grazing

Parking National Park car park beyond Fish Hotel (fee)

Public Toilets At start

1 Leave the car park and turn right, passing the Fish Hotel to follow a broad track through gates. Ignore the signposted route to Scale Force and continue along the track towards the edge of the lake. Then follow the line of a hedgerow to a bridge at Buttermere Dubs. Cross a small footbridge and go through a nearby gate in a wall at the foot of Burtness Wood and the cascade of Sourmilk Gill. Turn left on a track through the woodland that roughly parallels the lakeshore, finally emerging from the woodland near Horse Close, where a bridge spans Comb Beck.

2 Keep on along the path to reach a wall leading to a sheepfold and a gate. Go left through the gate, cross Warnscale Beck and walk out to Gatesgarth Farm. At the farm, follow signs to reach the valley road. A short stretch of road walking, left on the B5289, now follows, along which there are no pathways. Take care against approaching traffic.

3 As the road bends left, leave it for a lakeside footpath on the left. The path leads into a field, beyond which it never strays far from the shoreline and continues to a stand of Scots pine, near Crag Wood.

4 Beyond Hassnesshow Beck bridge, the path enters the grounds of Hassness, where a rocky path, enclosed by trees, leads to a gate. Here a path has been cut across a crag where it plunges into the lake below, and shortly disappears into a brief, low and damp tunnel, the only one of its kind in the Lake District. The tunnel was cut by employees of George Benson, a 19th-century mill owner who owned the Hassness Estate, so that he could walk around the lake without straying far from its shore. After you emerge from the tunnel a gate gives access to a gravel path across the wooded pasture of Pike Rigg. A path leads through a series of gates beyond the foot of the lake to a bridge of slate slabs.

5 A short way on, through another gate, the path leads on to Wilkinsyke Farm, and an easy walk out to the road, just a short way above the Bridge Hotel. Turn left to return to the car park.

65 Tarset, Thorneyburn and the Rievers Trail

Take a few hours' retreat on a woodland and moorland walk

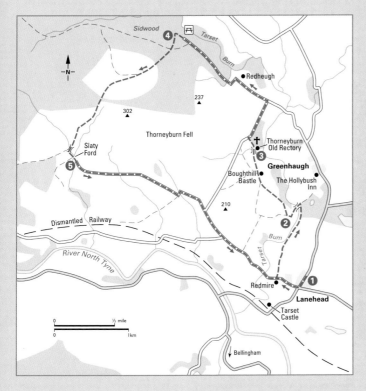

Distance 7.5 miles (12.1km)

Minimum Time 3hrs

Ascent/Gradient 1,083ft (330m) ▲▲▲

Level of Difficulty ●●●

Paths Burnside and moorland paths and tracks – some wet areas

Landscape Valleys with woodland and moorland

Suggested Map OS Explorer OL42 Kielder Water & Forest

Start/Finish Grid reference: NY 793858

Dog Friendliness Dogs on leads in farmland

Parking Beside Tarset Village Hall in Lanehead, on Greenhaugh road

Public Toilets None en route

1 Walk to the staggered crossroads in the middle of Lanehead and turn right, signed 'Donkleywood'. At the Redmire cottages turn right through a gate, and cross the yard to leave by two more gates. Cross the field, passing through a gap to reach a hand-gate. Bear left, descending to a kissing gate by the river. Follow the river bank right, through a series of gates before rising to a final gate and dropping to a bridge. Cross the Tarset Burn and follow the path down a ramp to join a farm track. Turn left along this to a farmyard.

2 Go though the farmyard and ascend the track on the far side. As it bears left, go ahead past a waymarker and downhill to cross the stream. Pass another waymarked post and go through a gateway. Bend right after it and go through a hand gate. Turn left along the fence, then, at a stile, bear half right across the open moor towards the woods and church. Keep left of the ruined wall, aiming for a dilapidated shed and a wall descending to a bridge over the burn.

3 Cross the stream. Veer left on the opposite bank to locate a gate at the side of a garden. Go through this and follow the track beside the churchyard to the road. Turn right and at the T-junction turn left. Follow the lane past Redheugh Farm and the 'Forestry Commission Sidwood' sign to Sidwood Picnic Area, near white-painted buildings.

4 Follow the path into the wood on the left, but after a short distance look for a right turn, crossing the burn and continuing up the hill. Cross a forest track and continue up the hill through an area of clear fell. Maintain your direction as the route levels out, now with a

ditch on your right. As you begin to descend, the forest gives way to moorland on your left and you reach a gate. Continue down through the enclosure, crossing a burn then rising to a crossing track. Turn left and follow this down to cross the burn with care at Slaty Ford.

5 Continue on this prominent enclosed track to a gate. Beyond this follow the minor road for a mile (1.6km) along the flank of the North Tyne valley passing through a gate after 0.5 mile (800m) to a junction. Keep ahead, over the cattle grid and down to the bridge over the Tarset Burn. Continue on this quiet lane as it ascends the bank back to the main road. Turn left to return to your car.

66 Derwent Valley's Past

Step back to when the Romans fortified Ebchester

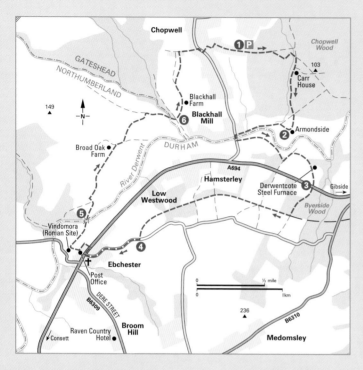

Distance 7 miles (11.3km)

Minimum Time 2hrs 30min

Ascent/Gradient 541ft (165m) ▲▲▲

Level of Difficulty ●●●

Paths Tracks, field paths and old railway line

Landscape Woodland and riverside, farmland and industrial remains

Suggested Map OS Explorer 307 Consett & Derwent Reservoir

Start/Finish Grid reference: NZ122579

Dog Friendliness On lead, except on former railway line

Parking Roadside parking in Chopwell; follow signs 'Chopwell Park Car Park'. Car park opens irregularly

Public Toilets None en route

1 Walk up the entrance road to Chopwell Park. Turn right past a metal barrier and bear right, into the wood. Follow the woodland track to a junction in about 200yds (183m). Pick out a narrow path on the right, marked by a wooden post amongst broom and gorse. Follow this winding path, eventually over a little bridge and up to join a forest road. Turn right, on to the road marked Forestry Commission road and follow the track downhill, passing Carr House on the left. The path drops down to the right and continues downhill. As the forest track swings right, turn left through a gate and continue down between the fields to Armondside Farm.

2 Bear right and follow the track to the road in Blackhall Mill. Turn left, over the bridge. Just beyond it, turn left by a footpath sign and follow the field-edge path to the right of the hedge. Follow the fenced riverside path. You may find there are some diversions along here

where the floods of September 2008 caused landslides. At a crossing path, turn left, uphill. At the top go sharp left, following waymark signs. Go left of the buildings, over a stile and across the field. Go over two wooden stiles then right. Follow the track uphill, passing Derwentcote Steel Furnace, to the main road.

3 Cross and take a signed footpath almost opposite. Go over a stile and, at a crossing path, turn right to another stile. Follow the path through woodland to the former railway track. Turn right and follow the track, which crosses another track (barriers at each side) and eventually rises to another barrier on to a metalled lane.

4 Turn right and descend into Ebchester. Bend right by the community centre to the main road. Cross over and turn right in front of the post office. Turn left at the footpath sign beyond. Follow the fence on your left, bend left

at the end beside the wall, follow the footpath downhill to a metalled lane. Turn right and continue until you reach a footbridge.

5 Cross the bridge. The footpath bends right before going straight ahead across the field to a stile. Follow the green lane uphill, pass a farmhouse and follow the track through several gates. Where the main track bears left, go straight ahead. Go through a gate and along the field-edge. Go though two gates to a T-junction of tracks.

6 Turn left, up the track towards a farm. About 300yds (274m) after the farm go right, through a gate and walk across the field to a stile, hidden in a hedge. Continue up the field to another stile right of the houses, and along a narrow lane. At the end, turn right along the tarmac lane. At the main road turn right and then left, following the signs 'Chopwell Park Car Park'.

67 The Wild Cattle of Chillingham Castle

Get close to the only wild cattle left in Britain

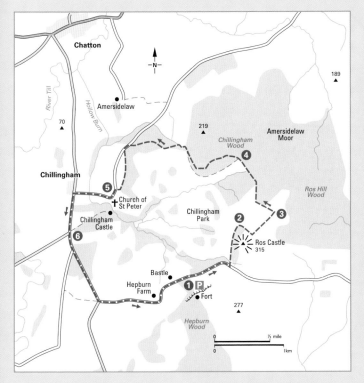

Distance 6 miles (9.7km)

Minimum Time 3hrs

Ascent/Gradient 754ft (230m) ▲▲▲

Level of Difficulty ●●●

Paths Hill track, surfaced road

Landscape Hill, arable and woodland

Suggested Map OS Explorer 340 Holy Island & Bamburgh

Start/Finish Grid reference: NU 071248

Dog Friendliness Dogs not allowed in Chillingham Wood, even on leads

Parking Forest car park at Hepburn Wood

Public Toilets None en route

1 On leaving the car park, turn right on the road and go uphill for 0.5 mile (800m) and round a bend to a National Trust notice indicating 'Ros Castle'. Follow the track to a gate in the wall to your left and go through the gate into Chillingham Wood. Turning right, and then going to the left, aim to follow marker posts on to a broader track after a distance of about 100yds (91m). This track leads you uphill, then across a level stretch to a fence. On your left is a view over Chillingham Park, where you might, on occasion, be able to see the wild cattle grazing.

2 Turn right at the fence and walk uphill as indicated by the signpost 'Chillingham'. When you reach the wall, turn to the left and follow the track between the wall and the fence to a picnic table. Continue to the next stretch of forest, and walk between the wall and the forest for about 250yds (229m) to the next signpost 'Chillingham'.

3 Turn left and descend through the forest, following the marker posts about 50yds (46m) apart. When this small track reaches a junction with a track signed 'Forest Walk', turn right and continue to a signpost. Take the Chillingham direction, through two tall kissing gates to a picnic area with two tables.

4 Continue along the track to a forest road and turn right on to this, which becomes metalled lower down. A sign points you left over a small bridge, back into the woods, following the red markers. The track rises to a gate in the deer fence, then levels off to run parallel with a wall. Continue beyond some picnic tables to a gate and then turn right. Keep right at the next junction, down the hill. Keep right again to descend to the road in front of Garden Cottage.

5 Turn left and follow the road past the Church of St Peter, on your left, then past a gate leading to Chillingham Castle. Cross the Hollow Burn either by ford or footbridge and continue to a T-junction with the main road. Turn left and follow the road, passing the main castle gate after 550yds (500m).

6 At the next fork in the road, go left uphill to the crossroads. This road is not very busy with traffic and has good grass verges for walking on. Turn left on the road to Hepburn Farm. Follow this, past the farm buildings, and continue to Hepburn Wood car park.

68 Berwick Town Walls

Explore old Berwick, then take a longer ramble beside the Tweed

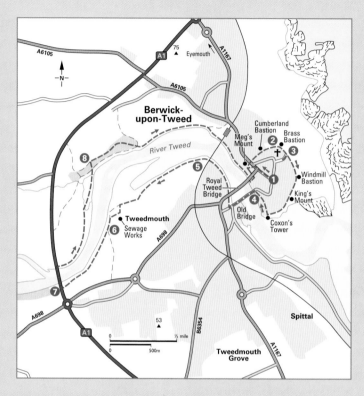

Distance 6.5 miles (10.4km)

Minimum Time 2hrs 15min

Ascent/Gradient 98ft (30m) ▲▲▲

Level of Difficulty ●●●

Paths Paved pathways and field paths; flood-meadows may be wet and muddy, particularly around high tide, 4 stiles

Landscape Town, riverside and woodland

Suggested Map OS Explorer 346 Berwick-upon-Tweed

Start/Finish Grid reference: NT 998529

Dog Friendliness On leads in town and near livestock

Parking Below ramparts outside Scots Gate

Public Toilets At car park, below ramparts

Note Sheer, unguarded drop from outer edge of town walls and bastions, keep to marked pathways

1 From the old Town Hall, walk west along Marygate to Scots Gate. Immediately before it, turn left to find a gateway on the right, where you can climb on to the walls by Meg's Mount. Follow the wall back over Scots Gate and on past the Cumberland Bastion.

2 The next battery, Brass Bastion, lies at the northern corner of the town. Some 100yds (91m) beyond, a path descends inside the wall to meet The Parade by the corner of the parish church graveyard. Turn right past the barracks to the church; both are worth visiting.

3 Return to the walls and go on, passing Windmill Bastion and the site of the earlier Edward VI fort. Beyond King's Mount, the walls rise above the Tweed Estuary before turning upriver at Coxon's Tower, past elegant Georgian terraces and on above the old quay.

4 Leave the walls at Bridge End and cross the Old Bridge. Turn right past the war memorial, go beneath the modern Royal Tweed Bridge and remain by the river beyond, shortly passing below Stephenson's railway viaduct.

5 The way continues upstream along a path. Where the bank widens to a rough meadow, pick up a track on the left, leading through a series of kissing gates to an open hide. A further gate leads out on to the next section of river bank. Beyond another gate, a contained path skirts a water treatment plant. Turn left through a second gate on to a tarmac track and turn right.

6 At a bend 40yds (37m) on, bear off right along a field-edge above the steep river bank. Continue in the next field but, towards its far end, look for a stepped path descending

the bank to a stream. Rising to a stile beyond, bear right to the main road.

7 Cross the Tweed and drop right on to a path, signed 'Berwick via Plantation', which crosses a couple of stiles to a riverside pasture. Walk away beside the left boundary for about 0.5 mile (800m). After crossing the head of a stream, move away from the hedge, aiming to meet the river below a wooded bank. Over a side bridge, bear right to a stile and continue through the trees beyond to a path at the top of the bank.

8 Go right, eventually dropping from the wood by a cottage, where a riverside promenade leads back to Berwick. Just beyond the Royal Tweed Bridge, turn sharp left, climbing back beneath it and continue beside the town walls to return to Meg's Mount.

Wales

A profoundly beautiful country with a fascinating history and culture, this is a land in which there is a strong desire to retain a local identity.

Wales is intrinsically rugged and wild. There are craggy heights, rock-strewn heather-clad hillsides, barren moors, bright green valleys, silver rivers and glassy mountain lakes, as well as rocky, storm-tossed coastlines with tumbling cliffs, picturesque coves and sublime golden beaches. And over it all lies a complex mantle of mystery and history. For walkers Wales has traditionally been a country of three parts – North, South and Mid-Wales. Each has its own distinctive character.

Much of walkers' North Wales is contained within the Snowdonia National Park, from time immemorial known to its inhabitants as Eryri, the 'Place of Eagles'. Eagles did once haunt the cliffs and cwms (steep-sided hollows) of North Wales. The popularity of Snowdon, the Carneddau, the Glyderau, the Rhinogs and the other mountains of Eryri has scarcely abated since the first recorded ascent of Snowdon in 1639 by botanist Thomas Johnson. The walks that follow pursue ancient footsteps and trackways from those of neolithic settlers on Anglesey (see Walk 85), to 1st-century tribes and their Roman conquerors in Snowdonia (see Walk 83).

Nor is the whole of North Wales Snowdonia. The eastern moorlands of Denbighshire flow westwards to the River Conwy below the eastern fringes of the Carneddau. On Walk 84 climb from Conwy for views of the estuary and town, and also of the Castell Caer Lleion fortress built by Iron Age settlers. North and west, the isle of Anglesey and the delectable Lleyn Peninsula boast renowned landscapes. On Anglesey admire the east coast of the island and visit the village of Moelfre (Walk 85). Further south, the Rhinogs are as rugged and rough as anything to be found in Britain.

One hundred years after the Domesday Book, Archbishop Baldwin of Canterbury began his mission to preach the Crusades in Wales in the quiet heartlands of Mid-Wales, at New Radnor, part of the great hunting Forest of Radnor. However, for the next two and a half centuries it was an unhappy, oppressed place, where the lords Marcher held power of life and death over the inhabitants, ruling them by sword under a severe form of martial law.

In the south, the Black Mountains (Mynyddoedd Duon) are a paradise for walkers who revel in long, lofty ridges separated by valleys of quiet calm. To the west rise the flat-topped summits of the Brecon Beacons, another Black Mountain (Mynydd Du) and the Fforest Fawr, names that speak of wilderness and desolation, and all contained within the Brecon Beacons National Park. Clamber up the Blorenge in Monmouthshire (Walk 71) for views both of the mountains and of Abergavenny and the former industrial area around it.

The further west you go, the greater the feeling of isolation. On the Gower peninsula Walk 70 delivers stunning views of Rhossili Bay. In North Pembrokeshire, brave the steep climbs and descents of the coastal path near Strumble Head for the reward of likely views of Atlantic seals (Walk 74). Isolation is never over-powering, for the seclusion works as a panacea for workaday ills; the wild, ponied expanses are among the most refreshing of ingredients in the panoply of Wales.

69 Island Views from the Marloes Peninsula

Tour a paddle-shaped peninsula that allows minimum inland walking for maximum time on the coast

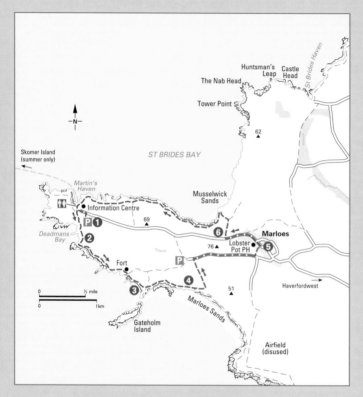

Distance 6 miles (9.7km)

Minimum Time 2hrs 30min

Ascent/Gradient 420ft (128m) ▲▲▲

Level of Difficulty ●●●

Paths Coast path and clear footpaths, short section on tarmac, 9 stiles

Landscape Rugged cliff tops and beautiful sandy beaches

Suggested Map OS Explorer OL36 South Pembrokeshire

Start/Finish Grid reference: SM 761089

Dog Friendliness Care near cliff tops and poop scoop on beaches

Parking National Trust car park above Martin's Haven, near Marloes village

Public Toilets Marloes village

1 From the bottom of the car park, walk down to the bottom of the hill. Bear around to the left, then go through the gate straight ahead into the Deer Park. Turn left and follow the path along to a gate and out on to the coast.

2 With the sea to your right, continue easily along over Deadmans Bay to a stile. The next section is easy walking, passing the earthworks of an Iron Age fort on the left and crossing another stile as you approach Gateholm Island.

3 It is possible to get across to the island at low tide, but care is needed to scramble over the slippery rocks. To continue the walk, follow the coast path above the western end of the beautiful Marloes Sands until you drop easily to the main beach access path.

4 Turn left and climb up to the road; turn right here. Follow the road along for around 0.75 mile (1.2km) to a hedged bridleway on the left. Follow this down and turn left into Marloes village.

5 Pass the Lobster Pot on the left and continue ahead to leave the village. Ignore tracks on the right, as the road bends to the left, and continue out into open countryside where you'll meet a footpath on the right.

6 Walk down the edge of the field and bear around to the left to descend to the coast path above Musselwick Sands. Turn left and follow the path west for 1.5 miles (2.4km) to Martin's Haven. Meet the road and climb past the information centre back to the car park.

70 The Highs and Lows of Rhossili Bay

Wonder, as you walk, at the stunning views over one of Wales's finest and wildest beaches

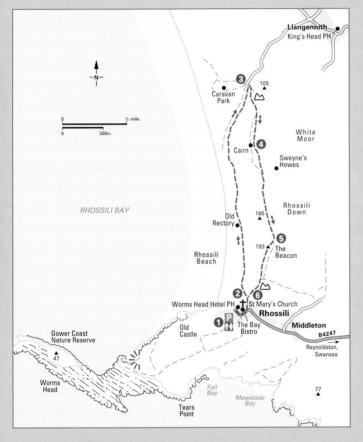

Distance 4 miles (6.4km)

Minimum Time 1hr 45min

Ascent/Gradient 590ft (180m) ▲▲▲

Level of Difficulty ●●●

Paths Easy-to-follow footpaths across grassy downs, 2 stiles

Landscape Rolling downland, rocky outcrops and views over gorgeous sandy beach

Suggested Map OS Explorer 164 Gower

Start/Finish Grid reference: SS 416880

Dog Friendliness Care needed near livestock

Parking Large car park at end of road in Rhossili

Public Toilets At start

1 From the car park, head out on to the road and continue uphill as if you were walking back out of the village. Immediately after passing St Mary's Church bear left down on a broad track to a gate at its end. Go through this and keep left to follow a grassy track that snakes along the steep hillside.

2 Follow this through the bracken, passing the Old Rectory on your left, and eventually you'll reach a sunken section with a wall on your left and a caravan park situated behind. Don't be tempted to break off right just yet; instead, keep going until you come to a gate on the left.

3 Don't go through the gate; turn sharp right and follow the grassy track steeply up on to the ridge. At the top of the steep section keep to the top track that follows the crest.

4 You'll pass some ancient cairns and drop slightly to pass a pair of megalithic cromlechs, or burial chambers. These are known as Sweyne's Howes and are more than 4,000 years old. Continue on a broad track up to the high point of The Beacon.

5 Keep straight ahead on a clear track that starts to drop easily then steepens to meet a dry-stone wall. Continue walking down the side of the wall and you'll eventually come to the gate you passed through on the way out.

6 Follow the lane out to the road, turn right and pass St Mary's Church on your right to return to the car park.

71 Bird's-eye View from the Blorenge

Enjoy a short sortie on to the hill that towers above the Beacons' eastern gateway

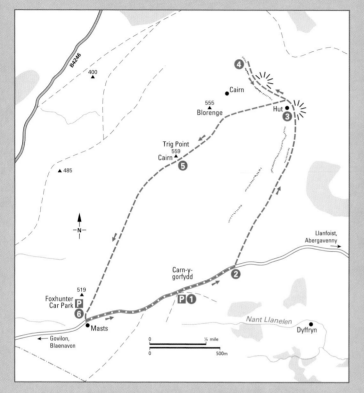

Distance 3 miles (4.8km)

Minimum Time 1hr 30min

Ascent/Gradient 530ft (161m) ▲▲▲

Level of Difficulty ●●●

Paths Clear tracks over open mountainside, quiet lane, no stiles

Landscape Rugged mountain scenery, huge views over Usk Valley

Suggested Map OS Explorer OL13 Brecon Beacons National Park Eastern area

Start/Finish Grid reference: SO 270109

Dog Friendliness Care needed near live-stock and on road

Parking Small car park at Carn-y-gorfydd

Public Toilets None en route

1 From Carn-y-gorfydd Roadside Rest, walk downhill for 500yds (457m) and bear left, through a green barrier, on to a grassy track.

2 This leads easily uphill, through a tangle of bracken, eventually allowing great views over the Usk Valley towards the outlying peak of Ysgyryd Fawr.

3 As the path levels you'll pass a small hut. Continue along the escarpment edge, on one of a series of terraces above the steep escarpment, and enjoy the views over Abergavenny and the Black Mountains. The rough ground was formed by stone quarrying.

4 Return to the hut and bear right, on to a faint, grassy track that crosses flat ground and a small boggy patch before climbing slightly and becoming stony. Away to the right, you should be able to make out the pronounced hump of a Bronze Age burial cairn. The path now leads easily to the trig point and the huge cairn that mark the summit.

5 Continue in the same direction, drop down past an impressive limestone outcrop and towards the huge masts on the skyline. You should also be able to see the spoil heaps on the flanks of Gilwern Hill, directly ahead.

6 At the masts, you'll cross the Foxhunter Car Park to meet the road where you turn left and continue easily downhill, for 600yds (549m), back to the start.

78 The 'Sublime' Mawddach

Cross the Mawddach estuary by historic footbridge for grand views of mountains, sand and water

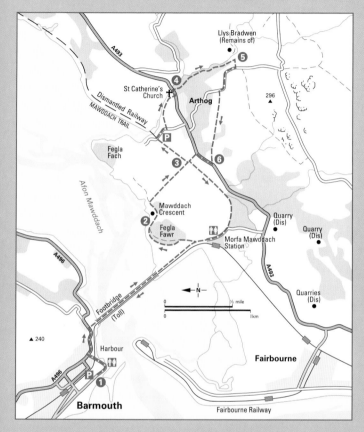

Distance 6 miles (9.7km)

Minimum Time 4hrs

Ascent/Gradient 656ft (200m) ▲▲▲

Level of Difficulty ●●●

Paths A bridge, good tracks and woodland paths, 6 stiles

Landscape Estuary and wooded hills

Suggested Map OS Explorer OL23 Cadair Idris & Llyn Tegid

Start/Finish Grid reference: SH 613155

Dog Friendliness Dogs should be on leads at all times

Parking Car park on seafront

Public Toilets At Barmouth's car park, or near Morfa Mawddach Station

1 Follow the promenade round the harbour, then go over the footbridge across the estuary (toll). On reaching the path along the south shore, turn left along the grassy embankment to a track rounding the wooded knoll of Fegla Fawr on its seaward side.

2 At the houses of Mawddach Crescent, take the track passing to their rear. Rejoin the track along the shoreline until you reach a gate on the right marking the start of a bridleway heading inland across the marshes of Arthog.

3 Turn left along the old railway track, then leave it just before the crossing of the little Arthog Estuary and turn right along a tarmac lane by a small car park. Bear left over a ladder stile and follow a raised embankment to a wall which now leads the path to the main Dolgellau road next to St Catherine's Church.

4 Opposite the church gate is a footpath beginning with steps into woodland. A waymarked path now climbs by the Arthog.

5 Beyond a stile at the top of the woods, turn right to a lane and right along the lane, then left along a track by the cottage of Merddyn. The track gets narrower and steeper as it descends into more woodland, beneath the boulders of an old quarry and down to the Dolgellau road by Arthog Village Hall.

6 Turn right along the road, then left along a path back to the railway track and the Mawddach Trail. Turn left along the trail and follow it past Morfa Mawddach Station and back across Barmouth's bridge.

79 Climbing With the Drovers Over the Roman Steps

Take one of Snowdonia's oldest pathways – but watch out for dangerous bogs if it has been raining

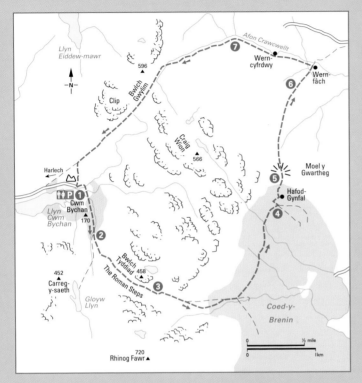

Distance 7 miles (11.3km)

Minimum Time 5hrs

Ascent/Gradient 1,575ft (480m) ▲▲▲

Level of Difficulty ●●●

Paths Rocky paths, tracks and boggy moorland, 9 stiles

Landscape Gnarled gritstone peaks with heather slopes

Suggested Map OS Explorer OL18 Harlech, Porthmadog & Bala

Start/Finish Grid reference: SH 646314

Dog Friendliness Can be off lead in upper heather-clad regions of walk

Parking Llyn Cwm Bychan

Public Toilets Portaloo at car par

Note The moorlands around the eastern end of the walk can be very wet and dangerous, with streams under the bogland. The walk is best tackled after a long dry spell

1 Go through the gate at the back of the car park at Llyn Cwm Bychan and over the paved causeway across the stream. Beyond a stile the path climbs up through woodland.

2 Over another stile you leave woodland behind and cross a stream on a small bridge. The path, always clear, climbs steadily to a gate. Now slabbed with 'the steps', it climbs through a heather-clad rocky ravine and on to the cairn marking the highest point along the rocky pass of Bwlch Tyddiad.

3 From the col, the path descends into a grassy moorland basin beneath Rhinog Fawr, then, beyond a stile, enters the conifers of the Coed-y-Brenin plantation. A well-defined footpath tucks away under the trees and eventually comes to a wide flinted forestry road, along which you turn left.

4 After about a mile (1.6 km), the road swings away to head east; watch out for a way-marked path on the left just beyond the turn. Waymarks guide the route left, then right, to pass the ruins of Hafod-Gynfal. Beyond this you head north to go over a ladder stile and out of the forest.

5 Go straight ahead from the stile, heading north across the grassy moor of Moel y Gwartheg. The ground gets wet as you descend, but it's wetter still further right. You're heading for the isolated cottage of Wern-fâch, which stands a little to the left of a small patch of conifers, but for now aim towards the green fields of Cefn Clawdd.

6 You meet a fence, which guides you down to Wern-fâch. Cross a stile, then just above the cottage turn left and go over two ladder stiles. Follow the main stream (Afon Crawcwellt) to Wern-cyfrdwy (house), pass behind it, then join the walls and fences that shadow the stream. These give the least wet line across the sodden moorland.

7 The going firms up as the ground steepens, climbing to the lonely col of Bwlch Gwylim, a narrow pass between Clip and Craig Wion. Descending the far side, Cwm Bychan and the start of the walk come back into view. The footpath now descends to the south-west, through heather and bracken. After a ladder stile, look for a small waymark where you turn left down steep slopes back to the car park.

80 In the Country of One of Wales's Most Famous Sons

Explore the coastal haunts of the last Liberal prime minister

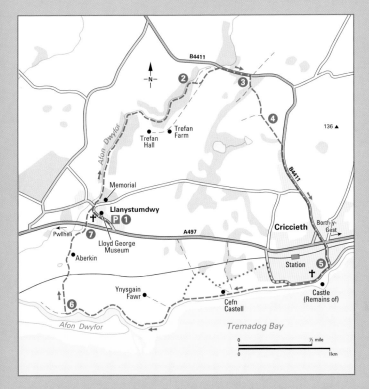

Distance 6 miles (9.7km)

Minimum Time 4hrs

Ascent/Gradient 300ft (91m) ▲▲▲

Level of Difficulty ●●●

Paths Generally well-defined paths and tracks, 4 stiles

Landscape Riverside woodland, fields, town streets, coastline

Suggested Map OS Explorer 254 Lleyn Peninsula East

Start/Finish Grid reference: SH 476383

Dog Friendliness Dogs can run free in riverside woods and on coast

Parking Large car park at east end of village

Public Toilets Near museum at Llanystumdwy and at Criccieth

Note Small section of coast path engulfed by highest tides. Make sure you know times of tides before setting off

1 Turn right out of the car park and go through Llanystumdwy village, past the museum to the bridge over the Afon Dwyfor. Turn right along the lane, then follow the footpath on the left past the memorial and down to the wooded river banks.

2 After 1.5 miles (2.4km) the path turns right, then goes under a stone archway to meet a tarred drive. Turn left along this, carry on to the B4411 and turn right.

3 After about 500yds (457m), turn right down an enclosed drive. As another drive merges from the left, turn half left along a path shaded by rhododendrons. After a few paces, go though the kissing gate, then cross the field guided by a fence on the left. Through another kissing gate the path veers half right, following a fence which is now on the right.

4 Beyond another gate the now sketchy route cuts diagonally (south-east) across two fields to rejoin the B4411 road, a mile (1.6km) or so north of Criccieth. Follow the B4411 into town. Keep straight on at the crossroads, and bear left after the level crossing to reach the promenade.

5 Follow the coast road past the castle and continue until it turns firmly inland. From here, tide permitting, simply follow the coast path or walk along the sands. Otherwise, follow the road to a bridleway on the left. Go past Muriau and then to the right of Ty Cerrig. Cross a track and a field then turn right on a green track, nearly to the railway. Head left, back to the coast path east of Ynysgain Fawr. Follow the coast path west through coastal grasslands and gorse scrub to the estuary of the Dwyfor and some crumbled concrete sea defences.

6 At a metal kissing gate, waymarks point inland. Follow these, with the fence on your right. The route becomes a farm track that cuts under the railway and passes through the yard of Aberkin farm before reaching the main road.

7 Cross the main road with care and go through the gate on the opposite side. A short path leads to an unsurfaced lane, which in turn leads to the village centre. Turn right for the car park.

81 Past the Horseshoe Falls to Climb Velvet Hill

Take a camera if you have one – the views make this one of the prettiest walks in the book

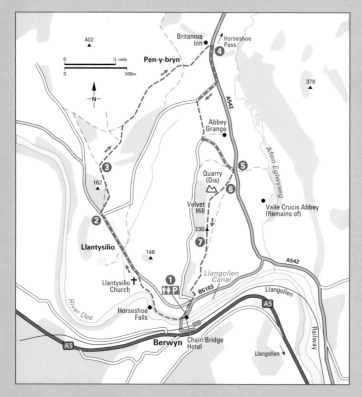

Distance 3.5 miles (5.7km)

Minimum Time 2hrs

Ascent/Gradient 902ft (275m) ▲▲▲

Level of Difficulty ●●●

Paths Field paths in valley and on hillside, 10 stiles

Landscape Rolling hillsides, woodland and riverside pastures

Suggested Map OS Explorer 255 Llangollen & Berwyn

Start/Finish Grid reference: SJ 198433

Dog Friendliness Farm pastures – dogs need to be on leads

Parking Picnic site and car park at Llantysilio Green on minor road north of Berwyn Station

Public Toilets At car park

1 From the car park walk down to the road, turn right for a few paces then descend steps to the back of the Chain Bridge Hotel. Turn right to follow the path between the river and the canal. Through a kissing gate at the end of the canal cross riverside fields past the Horseshoe Falls and climb to Llantysilio Church. On reaching the road, turn left through the hamlet of Llantysilio to reach a junction.

2 Continue a few paces further to find a stile on the right and then climb along a rutted track, which keeps a forest to the left, then climbs north on a high pastured hillside.

3 Over a stile at the top of the field the path swings right above a plantation. Keep right at a fork and later cross a stile before eventually descending to cottages at Pen-y-bryn. An enclosed path drops to a stile, which leads out to the Horseshoe Pass road at Britannia Inn.

4 Turn right along the road, then right again when you get to the first junction. At a bend, mount a stile on the left to head south across the fields. Reaching a farm track briefly go right, leaving at a fork over a stile on the left on to a narrow lane. Go left here to meet the Horseshoe Pass road again.

5 Go over a stile on the right-hand side of the road, signposted to the Velvet Hill, and ascend by quarry workings.

6 Later, swing right along a wide grassy track climbing steeply through bracken to reach the ridge, and go left for the summit.

7 Descend south on a narrow footpath to reach a fence above some woods. Do not cross (as many have done), but follow the fence down left to a stile. After crossing the stile go right, along a path that leads back to the lane near the car park.

82 A Sight of Bala's Gem – 'The Lake of Beauty'

Get the big – and boldly beautiful – picture on Llyn Tegid

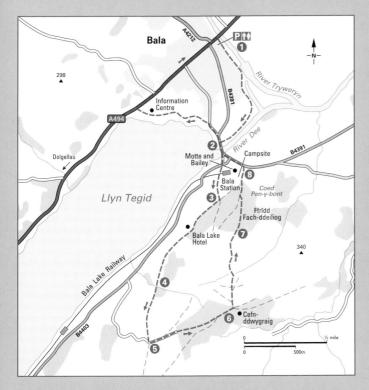

Distance 5 miles (8km)

Minimum time 3hrs

Ascent/Gradient 656ft (200m) ▲▲▲

Level of Difficulty ●●●

Paths Woodland and field paths, 7 stiles

Landscape Woods and upland pasture

Suggested Map OS Explorer OL23 Cadair Idris & Llyn Tegid, or OS Explorer OL18 Harlech, Porthmadog and Bala

Start/Finish Grid reference: SH 929361

Dog Friendliness Dogs should be on leads at all times

Parking Car park at entrance to Bala town from east

Public Toilets At car park

1 Go to the north corner of the car park in Bala to access the riverside path. Turn right to follow a raised embankment along the west bank of the Tryweryn. After a dog-leg to the right, passing through two kissing gates, the footpath continues, first by the banks of the Tryweryn, then by the north banks of the Dee.

2 On reaching the road, cross the bridge over the River Dee, then a smaller, older bridge. Go through a kissing gate to cross a small field to Bala Station on Bala Lake Railway. A footbridge allows you to cross the track before traversing two small fields.

3 Turn right along a cart track, and continue to pass behind the Bala Lake Hotel. A waymarker points the direction up a grassy bank on the left, and the path continues to a stile and then follows a fence on the right.

4 Descend slightly to cross a stream beside a small cottage, go up again then along a level fence to a stile. Bear left up through some bracken and wind up steeply at first, then continue more easily to a tarmac lane.

5 Turn left along the lane to a cattle grid from where you continue on a stony track, passing through felled plantations.

6 Just before the isolated house of Cefn-ddwygraig, turn left to a ladder stile. Follow a grass track across gorse-covered slopes. Keep left at a fork and drop down to a stile. The well-waymarked path continues north, with Bala town ahead.

7 Go over a partially hidden step stile into the commercial forestry plantations of Coed Pen-y-bont. A narrow footpath descends

to the bottom edge of the woods (ignore the forestry track you meet on the way down).

8 At the bottom of the woods turn right along a track that reaches the road by the Pen-y-Bont Campsite. Turn left along the road, cross the Dee again, bear left and then follow the lakeside footpath past the information centre. When you reach the main road, turn right to explore the fascinating town centre.

83 Ancient Stones and Settlements on Tal y Fan

See how Bronze and Iron Age settlers lived on the most northerly 2,000ft (610m) hill in Wales

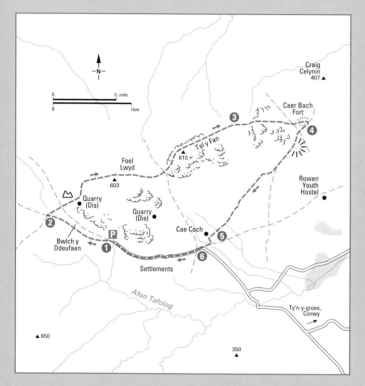

Distance 5 miles (8km)

Minimum Time 3hrs

Ascent/Gradient 984ft (300m) ▲▲▲

Level of Difficulty ●●●

Paths Cart tracks and narrow mountain paths, 7 stiles

Landscape Moor and mountain

Suggested Map OS Explorer OL17 Snowdon

Start/Finish Grid reference: SH 720715

Dog Friendliness Can be off lead on high ridges, but should be kept under tight control in farmland

Parking Car park at end of Bwlch y Ddeufaen road, off B5106 Conwy–Llanwrst road

Public Toilets None en route

1 From the car park at the top of the metalled section of the road to Bwlch y Ddeufaen, continue along the road, which is now unsurfaced, and follow it past the ancient standing stones to the high pass itself, where you go through a gate in a crossing wall.

2 Turn right and follow the course of the wall, across the pass under three lines of pylons, and then up the steep slopes of Foel Lwyd. A narrow footpath continues, first descending to a little saddle, or col, then climbing to the rockier summit of Tal y Fan.

3 The descending footpath follows the line of the dry-stone wall: when the wall turns right, go straight ahead, towards the hill of Craig Celynin. Thread between outcrops to reach a green valley running down to the right; look for the mound of Caer Bach Fort.

4 When you reach the remains of the fort turn right to follow a tumbledown wall heading south-west across high pastureland overlooking the Conwy Valley. Except for a short stretch this wall now acts as your guide, as do the frequent ladder stiles and locked gates sited in all the intervening cross-walls.

5 The footpath becomes a cart track, which passes beneath the whitewashed cottage of Cae Coch before turning left to join the stony vehicle track that has come from Rowen Youth Hostel.

6 Turn right along the track, which soon joins the Bwlch y Ddeufaen road at a sharp corner. Go straight ahead along the road and follow it back to the car park.

84 Conwy: Castle High and Castle Low

Take a tour from historic Conwy up to an outpost of the Celtic era

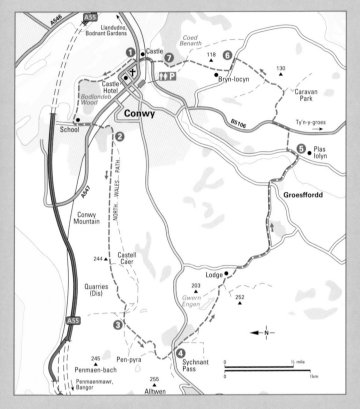

Distance 6.75 miles (10.9km)

Minimum Time 4hrs

Ascent/Gradient 1,493ft (455m) ▲▲▲

Level of Difficulty ●●●

Paths Good paths and easy-to-follow moorland tracks, 5 stiles

Landscape Town, coastline high ridge, farmland and copse

Suggested Map OS Explorer OL17 Snowdon

Start/Finish Grid reference: SH 783775

Dog Friendliness Can run free on high ridges, but keep on lead elsewhere

Parking Large car park on Llanrwst Road behind Conwy Castle

Public Toilets At car park

1 From Conwy Quay head north-west along the waterfront, going past the Smallest House and under the town walls. Next fork right along a tarmac waterside footpath that rounds Bodlondeb Wood. Turn left along the road, past the school and on to the A547. Cross the road, then go over the railway line by a footbridge. The track beyond the railway skirts a wood in order to reach a lane, and at this point you should turn right.

2 At a fork bear right past a house to a waymarked stile, from which a footpath makes its way up the wooded hillsides on to Mynydd y Dref (Conwy Mountain). Follow the undulating crest of Conwy Mountain and continue past the remains of the 10-acre (4ha) Castell Caer fortress.

3 Several tracks converge in the high fields of Pen-Pyra. Here, follow signposts for the 'North Wales Path' along the track heading to the south-west over the left shoulder of Alltwen and down to the metalled road traversing the Sychnant Pass.

4 Follow the footpath from the other side of the road, skirting the woods on your left. Climb over a stile, then carry on past Gwern Engen to meet a track. Go right on the track and then bear left, dropping above the Lodge to reach a lane. Turn right along the lane, then turn left, when you reach the next junction, into Groesffordd village. Cross the road, then take the road ahead that swings to the right past a telephone box, then left (south-east) towards Plas Iolyn.

5 Turn left at the end then opposite a white house take a path up to a cottage. Cross a track and go upfield to the B5106, then left to Conwy Touring Park. Follow the drive to a hairpin, take a waymarked path through trees, recrossing the drive. Through a kissing gate, go up the field-edge, then left along a ridge above successive pastures, finally meeting a lane.

6 Turn left, then right along a track past a communications mast to Bryn-locyn. Continue to a stile by Coed Benarth, from which a path drops beside the wood.

7 Go over a ladder stile on your left-hand side and across a field to a roadside gate. Turn right on to the B5106 to quayside, or turn left to get back to the main car park.

85 Moelfre and the Ancient Village

Enjoy bracing sea air and stirring coastal views before visiting Celtic remains on Anglesey

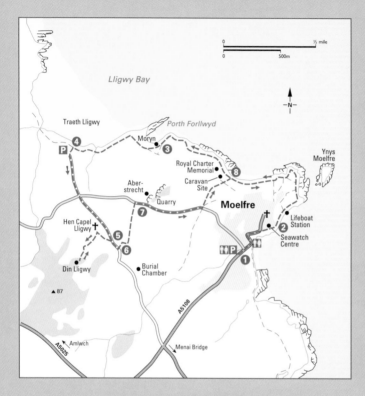

Distance 5 miles (8km)

Minimum Time 3hrs

Ascent/Gradient 541ft (165m) ▲▲▲

Level of Difficulty ●●●

Paths Well-defined coastal and field paths, 5 stiles

Landscape Sea cliffs and coastal pasture

Suggested Map OS Explorer 263 Anglesey East

Start/Finish Grid reference: SH 511862

Dog Friendliness Can be off lead on coastal path

Parking Car park at entrance to village

Public Toilets In car park and by harbour

1 From the car park, follow the main road (A5108) down to the shore. The road winds behind the bay before swinging left. Leave the road at that point for a shoreline path on the right.

2 Pass the the Seawatch Centre and the lifeboat station and ignore the footpath signs pointing inland. Instead follow a clear coast path that provides fine views across to the island of Ynys Moelfre. After passing to the right of some terraced cottages and going through a couple of kissing gates, the path crosses a small caravan site. It then goes through another kissing gate and climbs past the Royal Charter memorial.

3 Swinging left into Porth Forllwyd, the path ends beside a cottage, Moryn. Follow a track to a gate, turning before it along a fenced path into a field. Keep ahead to rejoin the coast, which turns in above the large bay of Traeth Lligwy.

4 On reaching the beach car park, turn left along the narrow lane before going straight ahead at the next crossroads.

5 Take the next path on the right, signposted to Din Lligwy ancient village. First, turn half right across the field to see the old chapel. Then bear left across two fields and into a wood concealing Din Lligwy. Return to the lane and turn right along it.

6 Leave after 50yds (46m) over a ladder stile on the left. Follow the dog-legging boundary right to a stile, over which turn left, walking downfield to emerge by a roadside quarry at Aber-strecht.

7 Follow the lane right to the edge of the village and go left on a waymarked track. Around the first bend, swing left through a gate, keeping right at a fork to walk through the caravan site again.

8 Follow the shoreline path retracing the outward route back to the car park at the start.

Scotland

Scotland offers the chance to see Britain's landscape on a grand scale along with a beautiful coastline and vast tracts of wilderness.

Scotland displays many faces, even on first acquaintance: the rolling hills of the Southern Uplands, the industrial urban belt between the Clyde and the Forth, then the Highlands in all their splendour, breaking up west and north into a succession of headlands and sea lochs, islands and stacks. There is a greater degree of freedom to roam than elsewhere, and a distinct culture and tradition evident wherever you travel. For this is a country with a history, law and culture all its own, but one whose affairs have been inextricably linked over centuries with those of Ireland and England – to say nothing of a profound Nordic influence.

Almost wherever you look, you can find evidence of strife. Largs (1263), Bannockburn (1314), Stirling Bridge (1297) and Culloden (1746) were all great and decisive battles. There are many sobering but fascinating reminders of these conflicts. At Wigtown (see Walk 86) you can walk in the footsteps of two women Covenanters martyred by government troops. On the Pentland Hills near Edinburgh (see Walk 91) you will be near the site on which a Covenanter army was defeated.

Yet there were also many great and stirring adventures. Legends developed around the exploits of cattle rustlers in the Highland clans. At the 'Corrie of Booty' (see Walk 96) the MacDonalds hid their stolen cattle, while at the Devil's Beef Tub (see Walk 89) the Johnstone Clan concealed their purloined animals.

Around Balquhidder you can investigate the tale of notorious Highland outlaw Rob Roy MacGregor, hero of Sir Walter Scott's 1817 novel *Rob Roy*, and even track down his burial place (see Walk 95). On the Rothiemurcus Estate near Aviemore in the Highlands, the island castle of Loch an Eilein stood close to a cattle-rustling route – known as 'Robbers' Way' – through the Rothiemurcius Forest used by Rob Roy and others (see Walk 100). The castle was the scene of brutal conflict between clans.

The walk at Loch an Eilein is of great interest to birdwatchers as well to those with a taste for Highland history. At Portree Bay (see Walk 101), there's a wonderful opportunity to see the white-tailed eagle and at Rogie Falls (see Walk 102) you may see a wild salmon. Near Caelaverock Caslte (see Walk 87), there's a splendid nature reserve.

The first rough highways through the glens and high passes were trodden by drovers, and the first attempt to establish a real road network came under the auspices of General Wade after the 1745 Jacobite Rebellion. Scotland soon developed a thriving tourism: no doubt its appeal was developed by the enthusiastic writings of native Scotsmen and visitors alike. And so it became a country with a great literary tradition, from ancient bards through Robert Burns and Sir Walter Scott (Walk 95) to Alasdair Gray or Alan Warner in the contemporary era. In Edinburgh a delightful walk in the New Town (Walk 93) celebrates the memory of writers with connections to that city, authors as diverse as the poet Shelley and Sherlock Holmes creator Sir Arthur Conan Doyle, or First World War poet Wilfred Owen.

86 On the Trail of the Wigtown Martyrs

Stand where two Scottish women lost their lives for defying an English king

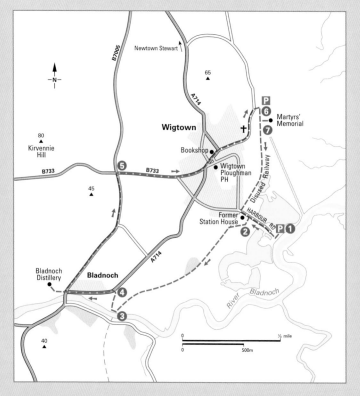

Distance 4 miles (6.4km)

Minimum Time 3hrs

Ascent/Gradient 98ft (30m) ▲▲▲

Level of Difficulty ●●●

Paths Roads, old railway tracks and pavements

Landscape River estuary, pasture and woodland

Suggested Map OS Explorer 311 Wigtown, Whithorn & The Machars

Start/Finish Grid reference: NX 439547

Dog Friendliness Keep on lead near livestock

Parking At Wigtown harbour

Public Toilets None on walk

1 Leave the car park, turn right and then head uphill on a narrow country lane called Harbour Road. The house situated on the left near the top of the road was the former station house for Wigtown. Just before it you will see a farm gate on the left. Go through the gate and on to a farm track.

2 Follow the track to the point where it goes through another gate then veer right and climb up the old railway embankment. This has a good grassy surface along its entire length. Proceed along the length of the embankment.

3 A wall across the track will stop you at the point where the former railway bridge carried the track across the River Bladnoch. Turn right and go down the side of the embankment and cross a gate into a field. Veer

right and head across the field to the far corner then go through a gate on to the main road.

4 Turn left and walk through the hamlet of Bladnoch. At the junction by a roundabout, cross the road to enter the Bladnoch Distillery car park. After visiting the distillery head back out of the car park and turn left at the roundabout. Continue along this road (the B7005) for approximately 1 mile (1.6km) until you get to a crossroads.

5 Turn right on to the B733 road and walk along it to reach Wigtown. When you reach the centre of the town bear left around the square and head towards the large and impressive former county buildings. Pass them on your right, then carry on past the church and war memorial on your left and continue

downhill. Eventually turn right into the car park for the Martyrs' Memorial.

6 Walk through the car park and then turn right and head along the path leading to the Martyrs' Memorial. Turn left and walk out over the sands on a specially constructed wooden causeway to reach the poignant memorial erected on the spot where the two women were drowned.

7 Return to the path and turn left. Go through a kissing gate then another gate, slightly below the level you are walking on and to the left. At the end of the path go through another gate in front of the station house, turn left on to Harbour Road to the car park.

87 Caerlaverock Castle and the Solway Merses

See seasonal birds in the reserve – and bring a picnic to eat at the castle

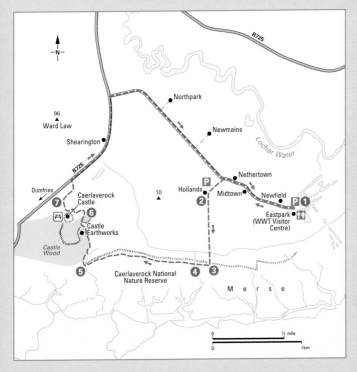

Distance 5.25 miles (8.4km)

Minimum Time 2hrs 30min

Ascent/Gradient 82ft (25m) ▲▲▲

Level of Difficulty ●●●

Paths Country lanes, farm tracks and salt marsh, 1 stile

Landscape Pastures, salt marsh, riverside and hills

Suggested Map OS Explorer 314 Solway Firth

Start/Finish Grid reference: NY 051656

Dog Friendliness Keep on lead while on reserve

Parking Car park at Wildfowl and Wetlands Trust Reserve

Public Toilets At Wildfowl and Wetlands Trust Reserve

1 Exit the car park and turn right on to a farm road. Follow this past the farms of Newfield and Midtown, then turn left and go past a bungalow and some houses. Just before the farm of Hollands there is a waymarker pointing to a car park on the right, and straight ahead for walks. Go straight ahead and continue to the farm steading, then turn left.

2 Go through a gate and on to a farm track. This stretches away into the distance and has high hedges on both sides. Continue along this track between the hedges and on, over an overgrown section, until you reach the end, then turn right when you reach the signpost indicating 'Caerlaverock'.

3 A sign here informs visitors that regulated wildfowling (shooting) takes place between 1 September to 20 February. Follow the rough track through the grass along the edge of the merse in the direction of the arrow on the footpath waymarker post. The path can be very boggy at all times and the grass will be high in the summer.

4 The path through the nature reserve varies from faint to non-existent; Wellington boots are recommended for all. It splits at several points and then meanders back and forth, but all the lines of the path rejoin and you'll end up at the same place whichever one you decide to take.

5 Eventually some cottages can be seen in the field to the right. Bear right, going through a gate and into the field. Walk to the left around the field perimeter, past some cottages, then take a left turn through a gate to emerge on to a farm track, passing a sign for 'Caerlaverock Castle' and going into the castle grounds.

6 Follow the road past the old castle, which has been excavated and has information boards to explain the ruins, and go through a wood with nature trail information boards to Caerlaverock Castle. There is a children's playground, a siege machine and picnic tables around the ramparts of the castle.

7 At the far end go through an arch and continue to the T-junction with a country lane. Turn right and continue for about a mile (1.6km), then turn right on to another lane signposted 'Wildfowl and Wetlands Reserve'. Continue on this road past the farms of Northpark, Newmains and Nethertown and then return to the car park at Eastpark.

88 Byne Hill and the Island of Ailsa Craig

Climb Byne Hill for one of the finest views over the Firth of Clyde to be had anywhere

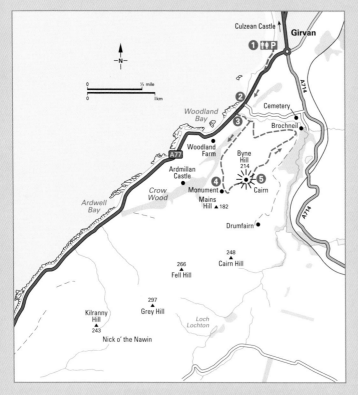

Distance 3.75 miles (6km)

Minimum Time 3hrs

Ascent/Gradient 571ft (174m) ▲▲▲

Level of Difficulty ●●●

Paths Farm roads, dirt tracks and open hillside, 1 stile

Landscape Hill, pasture, woodland and seaside

Suggested Map OS Explorer 317 Ballantrae, Barr & Barrhill

Startf/Finish Grid reference: NX 187955

Dog Friendliness Keep on lead, this is sheep country

Parking Ainslie Park car park

Public Toilets At the car park

1 From the car park head south along a pavement alongside the A77. Pass a nursing home on the right, then come to a lane on the left past former Shalloch mill.

2 The pavement disappears so continue along the verge for 200yds (183m). Just before it reappears cross a bridge, then turn left and cross the road.

3 Go on to a farm track that runs alongside a burn. Go over a metal gate and turn right. Follow this newly created road, which runs behind Woodland Farm and Ardmillan Castle Holiday Park. There are several metal gates to go through along the way. Please take careful notice of these – ensure that you always close them behind you while leaving open any that are not closed.

4 Continue on to the saddle between Mains Hill on your right-hand side and Byne Hill on your left, passing the remains of a monument that was erected to the memory of Archibald C B Craufurd of Ardmillan Estate. As the monument is in poor repair keep a safe distance from it. There used to be a plaque on the front, but some years ago this was removed and dumped in the woods below. Turn left through a gap in the wall and head up the side of Byne Hill to reach a prominent commemorative cairn at the summit. From this vantage point there is one of the finest views available of the Firth of Clyde. On a clear day you can see the Antrim coast of Northern Ireland, the island of Arran and the Mull of Kintyre to the north and west, and, about 8 miles (12.9km) out in the sea, the distinctive outline of Ailsa Craig.

5 With the cairn at your back, walk straight ahead. Cross a saddle between the summit and the lower part of the hill, keeping at first to the higher ground then towards the north side of the hill. Descend very carefully and at the bottom, turn left and follow the wall. Continue until you pass a gate then turn right over a stile and cross the field to then go over the gate on to the farm road at Point 3. From here retrace your steps to the start.

89 A 'Beefy' Devil of a Walk in Moffat

Tour a cattle-rustlers' hideout that was later a natural sanctuary for religious dissenters

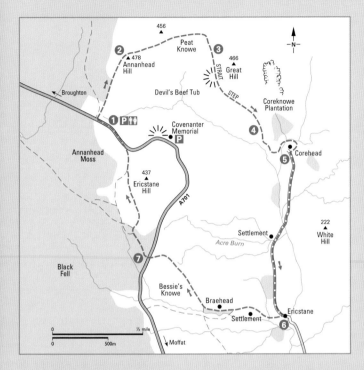

Distance 4.5 miles (7.2km)

Minimum Time 2hrs

Ascent/Gradient 1,076ft (328m) ▲▲▲

Level of Difficulty ●●●

Paths Farm tracks, small paths; narrow path across steep Beef Tub slope

Landscape Dramatic Beef Tub hollow and views of the Borderlands

Suggested Map OS Explorer 330 Moffat & St Mary's Loch

Start/Finish Grid reference: NT 057128

Dog Friendliness Keep on lead when passing sheep and cattle

Parking Lay-by just south of forest gateway

Public Toilets Lay-by just south of forest gateway

Warning Bull with cows occasionally at Point 4

1 Walk up the A701 to the forest gateway on the right. Don't take the wide gravel track, but a wooden gate on the right-hand side, to a small path to the left of a fence. Climb rails at a fence end, and head up the grassy slope of Annanhead Hill, keeping to the right of the plantation area to the trig point on the summit.

2 The small path continues around the flank of Peat Knowe, keeping the wall and fence to your left. Follow the path down the grassy slope of Annanhead Hill, keeping to the head of a gully, where your path meets the wall. Walk to the other side of the gully.

3 Past the gully head, turn right on a small path that runs just above, and to the left of, the grassy gully. As the slope drops away steeply, the path, called Strait Step, bends left and contours on a level line across the steep slope, below some small craggy outcrops. As

the slope eases, the path slants down through bracken, heading towards the Coreknowe plantation at the valley end. Just before the plantation, you'll reach a metal gate leading into a field.

4 A bull occasionally grazes in this field, so if you need to avoid him, pass along above the field and climb an awkward fence into the plantation. Slant down to the right, under the trees, as far as a gate into the field with the tiny footbridge mentioned below. Otherwise, go through the grey gate and down along beside a grassy bank. Turn left on a rough track that leads to the bottom corner of the plantation. The track reaches a gate above a red-brick house. Through the gate, following signs for 'Moffat', head out into the field to a tiny footbridge, then bear right to pass to the left of the white buildings of Corehead farm. A fence on the right leads to a gate on to the farm's access track.

5 Follow the farm road along the bottom of the valley. The small area of undulating land visible on the right is the remains of an ancient settlement.

6 After a cattle grid, at the start of the buildings, turn up right through a gate signed 'footpath'. A stony track leads past a house and through a gate. Turn right, following the track as it runs above a stone wall. Eventually you'll reach the main A701. Cross over – taking care, because the road is often busy – on to a rough track opposite.

7 The route passes over Ericstane Hill. Bear right and follow the track as it runs north round the far side of the hill. On open hill, the track is indistinct, deep ruts half-hidden under rushes. Pass through a slight col to the left of the hill summit, to rejoin the A701. Turn right here to visit the Covenanter memorial, or turn left to return to the start of the walk.

90 Alexander 'Greek' Thomson

Discover the beauties of a Victorian city and the architect who shaped it

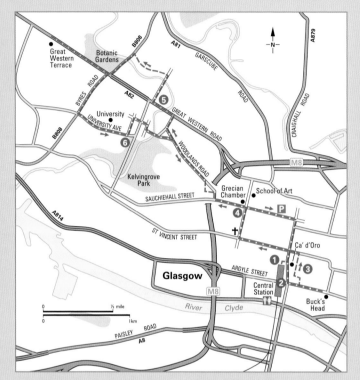

Distance 6.5 miles (10.4km)

Minimum Time 3hrs 30min

Ascent/Gradient 98ft (30m) ▲▲▲

Level of Difficulty ●●●

Paths Pavements

Landscape City streets

Suggested Map OS Explorer 342 Glasgow; AA Street by Street Glasgow

Start/Finish Grid reference: NS 587653

Dog Friendliness Not great walk for dogs

Parking Sauchiehall Street multi-storey or on-street parking

Public Toilets At Central Station

1 Exit Central Station and turn right. At the junction with Union Street turn right. The building on the opposite corner is the Ca' d'Oro building, a late 19th-century Italianate warehouse by John Honeyman, based on the Golden House in Venice. The upper storeys are made of cast iron. A little way down Union Street from here on the same side as the Ca' d'Oro is Thomson's Egyptian Halls, sadly in need of some renovation.

2 Cross over then head down Union Street turning left into Argyle Street at the next junction. Cross Argyle Street, then walk to the junction with Dunlop Street, where you will find the Buck's Head building named after an inn that once stood on this spot. Cross Argyle Street again, retrace your steps, turning right into Buchanan Street. Turn left into Mitchell Lane, pass the Lighthouse, then turn right.

3 Walk up Mitchell Street, continue along West Nile Street then turn left into St Vincent Street. Continue on this for just under 0.5 mile (800m), going uphill to the junction with Pitt Street. You are now standing in front of Alexander 'Greek' Thomson's St Vincent Street Church, one of his greatest achievements. Cross St Vincent Street here then head up Pitt Street to Sauchiehall Street.

4 On the opposite corner is Thomson's Grecian Chamber (1865) and to the right along Scott Street is Rennie Mackintosh's Glasgow School of Art. From the front of the Grecian Chamber turn left, head down Sauchiehall Street to Charing Cross, then take the pedestrian bridge over the motorway to Woodlands Road. Go along this until it ends at Park Road, then turn right before turning left again into Great Western Road.

5 Go right on Belmont Street, left at Doune Gardens, continue along Doune Quadrant, then left again at Queen Margaret Drive. Cross the road and head down past the Botanic Gardens to turn right, back into Great Western Road. Cross the road and continue to Great Western Terrace, another Thomson masterpiece. Retrace your steps back from here to the top of Byres Road and turn right then, near the bottom, turn left into University Avenue.

6 Go left into Oakfield Avenue, pass Eton Terrace on the corner with Great George Street. Turn right into Great George Street, right at Otago Street, left into Gibson Street and keep going when it becomes Eldon Street. Turn right into Woodlands Road and return to Sauchiehall Street. Follow this to the junction with Renfield Street, turn right and head downhill to Central Station.

91 Soldiers and Saints on the Pentlands

Get away from it all in peaceful countryside just beyond the Edinburgh city bypass

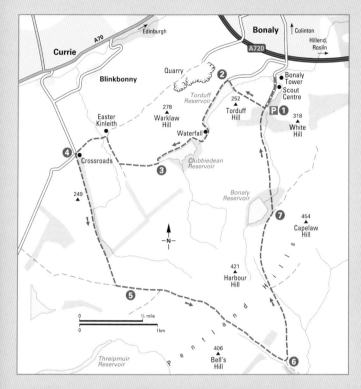

Distance 7 miles (11.3km)

Minimum Time 3hrs

Ascent/Gradient 837ft (255m) ▲▲▲

Level of Difficulty ●●●

Paths Wide firm tracks, short stretches can be muddy, 3 stiles

Landscape Reservoirs, fields and hills

Suggested Map OS Explorer 344 Pentland Hills

Start/Finish Grid reference: NT 212679

Dog Friendliness Good, but beware of ground-nesting birds

Parking Car park at end of Bonaly Road, beyond Bonaly Tower

Public Toilets None en route

1 From the car park, go through the gate and take the right-hand path, signposted 'Tordruff Reservoir'. Beyond a wooden gate, the path crosses over the reservoir dam to intersect with a tarmac lane.

2 Turn left along the lane, keeping Tordruff Reservoir on your left-hand side. When you reach the top of the reservoir, walk over the little bridge and follow the metalled track as it bends round to the right beside a waterfall. Walk under a line of electricity pylons, and go over a small bridge, passing a water chute on your left-hand side, and continue past Clubbiedean Reservoir.

3 Your path now bears right, with fields on either side. Pass under another line of pylons and walk to Easter Kinleith farm. Now follow the lane as it bends back to the left,

signposted 'Harlaw'. Pass a sign for 'Poets' Glen' and continue ahead, walking over a bridge and on to a large white house on the left-hand side called Crossroads.

4 Turn left. Follow the track past a conifer plantation situated on your left-hand side, then go through a small gate. Continue walking ahead until you reach an intersection of ways. Turn left through a gate, which is signposted 'Glencorse'.

5 Follow the path across the moorland and on up into the hills, carrying on until you come to a stone stile. Cross the stile and then continue in the same direction until you come to a copse of conifers standing on the right-hand side, with Glencorse Reservoir visible ahead. Turn left at this point, following the sign 'Colinton by Bonaly'.

6 Walk uphill and maintain direction to go through a metal gate. The track now narrows and takes you through the hills, until it eventually opens out. Continue in the same direction to reach a fence encircling conifers. Keep the fence on your left and walk down to a gate on the left-hand side.

7 Turn left through the gate. Walk past Bonaly Reservoir, then through a kissing gate and walk downhill, getting good views over Edinburgh as you descend. When you reach a wooden gate, go through and continue ahead, walking downhill, with trees on either side. Go through another kissing gate and follow the tarmac path ahead to return to the car park and the start of the walk.

92 The Romance of Roslin Glen

See the Scottish chapel that has become a movie star

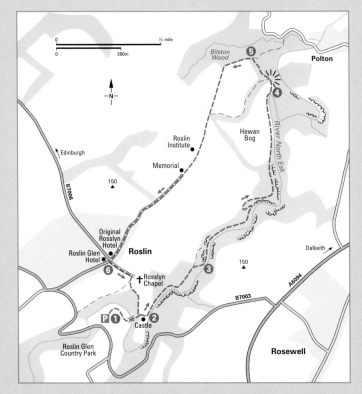

Distance 5 miles (8km)

Minimum Time 2hrs 30min

Ascent/Gradient 279ft (85m) ▲▲▲

Level of Difficulty ●●●

Paths Generally good, but can be muddy and slippery

Landscape Woodland and fields, short sections of road

Suggested Map OS Explorer 344 Pentland Hills

Start/Finish Grid reference: NT 272627

Dog Friendliness Can mostly run free, steps and climbs might not suit some

Parking Roslin Glen Country Park car park

Public Toilets None en route; nearest at Rosslyn Chapel Visitor Centre

1 From the country park car park, walk north-east with the sound of the river through the trees to your left. Go up the metal stairs, cross the footbridge, then walk ahead, following the path uphill. In summer, the smell of wild garlic will soon waft over you. At the bottom of a flight of steps, turn right, walk under the old castle arch, down some stone steps, then turn to your left.

2 Follow the path through scrub and up some steps, going ahead into dense woodland. When you reach a muddy burn, bear left, keeping to the main path with the gorge to your right. Beyond a line of yew trees growing from an old stone wall, take a right turn and follow the path that winds steeply downhill until you reach the water's edge.

3 Walk to your left, then follow the path as it climbs again. At a crossing of paths turn right, following the direction of the river. Your way now takes you high above the river, and you continue ahead to cross a stile. After you cross another stile the view opens out to fields on your left, then takes you closer to the river again, until you reach a kissing gate.

4 Turn left and follow the path up steps with fields to your left. When you reach the top of the ridge there are good views to your right. Continue until you go through a kissing gate

5 Turn left and follow the wide path. You eventually walk past buildings of the Roslin Institute, where Dolly the sheep was cloned, then pass a memorial to the Battle of

Rosslyn on your right-hand side. Keep walking straight ahead, through the outskirts of Roslin and up to the crossroads at the village centre.

6 Turn left here and walk ahead. After a short distance you see Rosslyn Chapel on the right-hand side. The chapel is well worth closer inspection. If you don't intend to visit the chapel, take the path that bears downhill to the right, just in front of it. When you reach the cemetery turn left, following the signpost for Polton, and walk between the cemeteries to the metal gate for Rosslyn Castle. Go down the steps on the right-hand side, over the bridge again and return to the car park at the start.

93 Edinburgh's Elegant and Airy New Town

Take a walk in the footsteps of literary giants

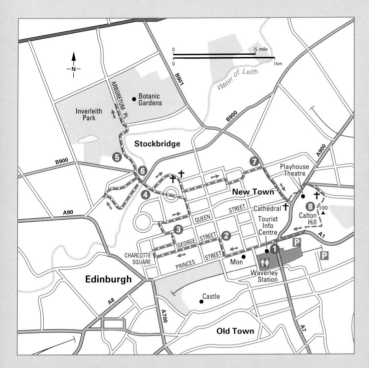

Distance 3 miles (4.8km)

Minimum time 1hr 30min

Ascent/Gradient 164ft (50m) ▲▲▲

Level of Difficulty ●●●

Paths Busy city streets

Landscape Elegant Georgian townscape

Suggested Map AA Street by Street Edinburgh

Start/Finish Grid reference: NT 257739

Dog Friendliness Keep on lead, not allowed in Botanic Gardens

Parking Several large car parks in central Edinburgh

Public Toilets At Waverley Station

1 From the tourist information centre, turn left and walk along Princes Street. Just after you pass the Scott Monument on your left, cross the road to reach Jenners department store, Scotland's answer to Harrods. Continue along Princes Street, then take a right turn up Hanover Street.

2 Take the second turning on your left and walk along George Street to reach elegant Charlotte Square. Then turn right and right again to go along Young Street. At the end, turn left and walk down North Castle Street to reach Queen Street.

3 Cross the road, turn left, then right down Wemyss Place and right into Heriot Row. When you reach Howe Street turn left and, before you reach the church in the middle of the street, turn left and walk along South East Circus Place. Walk past the sweep of Royal Circus and then down into Stockbridge.

4 Cross the bridge, then turn left along Dean Terrace. At the end, turn right into Ann Street. When you reach Dean Park Crescent turn right and follow the road round into Leslie Place and into Stockbridge again. Cross the main road, turn left and then right at the traffic lights down St Bernard's Row. Follow this, then bear left into Arboretum Avenue.

5 Follow this road past the Water of Leith down to Inverleith Terrace. Cross and walk up Arboretum Place to reach the entrance to the Botanic Gardens on the right. Turn left after exploring the gardens and retrace your steps to Stockbridge again.

6 Turn left at Hectors bar and walk uphill, then turn left along St Stephen Street. When you reach the church follow the road, cross over Cumberland Street then turn left and continue along Great King Street. At the end, turn right, then immediately left to walk along Drummond Place, past Dublin Street and continue ahead into London Street.

7 At the roundabout turn right and walk up Broughton Street to reach Picardy Place. Turn left, walk past the statue of Sherlock Holmes, then bear left towards the Playhouse Theatre. Cross over, continue left, then turn right into Leopold Place and right again into Blenheim Place. When you reach the church turn right, walk up the steps and turn left at the meeting of paths.

8 Go up the steps on the right, walk over Calton Hill, then turn right to pass the canon. Go downhill, take the steps on your left and walk down into Regent Road. Turn right and walk back into Princes Street and the start.

94 The Stones of Kilmartin Church and Glen

See ancient stones and burial sites in the grandeur of their natural setting

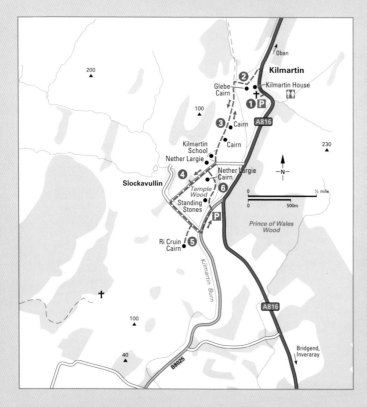

Distance 3.5 miles (5.7km)

Minimum Time 3hrs

Ascent/Gradient Negligible ▲▲▲

Level of Difficulty ●●●

Paths Boggy fields, old coach road and country lanes, 3 stiles

Landscape Pasture, hills, woodland

Suggested Map OS Explorer 358 Lochgilphead & Knapdale North

Start/Finish Grid reference: NR 835988

Dog Friendliness Dogs fine on route

Parking Car park outside Kilmartin Church

Public Toilets Kilmartin House

1 From the car park visit Kilmartin Church to spend a little time inspecting the medieval gravestones and to see the exquisite Kilmartin Cross. When you have finished and are leaving the church, turn left and walk along the road past Kilmartin House, walk out of the village and begin to head downhill towards a garage on the left. Just before the garage turn left, go through a kissing gate and head across the field to the Glebe Cairn.

2 From the cairn head half right across the field to climb over a stile. In wet weather this area can be very boggy, so stout footwear is advisable. Cross the stream by a bridge, then go on through a gate and take a left turn on to the old coach road. Follow this coach road to the next cairn. Go left over a stile and follow the path to visit the cairn.

3 Return to the road and turn left, continuing to the next cairn. After exploring this cairn, follow the coach road to Kilmartin School, where the route becomes a metalled road. Go over a crossroads, then walk on past Nether Largie Farm and, ignoring the cairn on the left, continue for a short distance towards Temple Wood, which is clearly visible ahead on the right.

4 Go through a gate on the right into Temple Wood, and when you have finished return by the same route. Turn right on to the road and continue until you reach a T-junction. Turn left at the junction and walk along this road until you come to a sign on the right for 'Ri Cruin Cairn'. Cross the wall by way of a stile and then proceed along the well-defined path to visit the ancient monument.

5 Return by the same route and turn right on to the road. Follow it to a T-junction then turn left and keep straight ahead until you reach the car park at Lady Glassary Wood. Opposite this take a path to the left signposted 'Temple Wood'. Cross a bridge, go through a gate and head towards the standing stones.

6 Turn right and walk across the field away from the stones towards a wood. Go through a gate and follow the fenced path to Nether Largie Cairn. From here continue along the fenced path, go through another gate and turn right on to the road. Continue past Nether Largie Farm and Kilmartin School and then retrace your steps back to reach Kilmartin Church and the car park.

95 From Balquhidder to Creag an Tuirc

Pay your respects at the grave of the Highlands' most famous outlaw

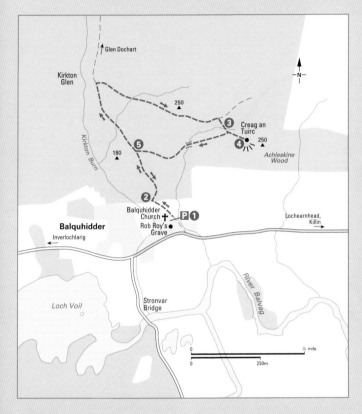

Distance 2.5 miles (4km)

Minimum Time 2hrs

Ascent/gradient 328ft (100m) ▲▲▲

Level of Difficulty ●●●

Paths Forest roads and hillside, 2 stiles

Landscape Hills, loch and woodlands

Suggested Map OS Explorer 365
The Trossachs

Start/Finish Grid reference: NN 536209

Dog Friendliness Dogs ok on this route

Parking At Balquhidder Church

Public Toilets None en route

1 The walk starts at the car park at Balquhidder Church. From here, walk along a dirt track, go past a shed and turn on to a path on the right-hand side that gives access into the forest. Follow the direction arrows on the green signposts pointing to 'Creag an Tuirc', along a forest track and heading up the hill.

2 Continue on this obvious trail for about 0.5 mile (800m) and then turn right, alongside a green building, again following the clearly signposted and waymarked route along a forest road. After walking for another 0.5 mile (800m), go through a gate on the right-hand side, then carry on walking slightly downhill over some stone steps and then go across a small stream.

3 The path now heads uphill on some stone steps, through old pine trees and on towards the summit of a knoll. Here is a cairn erected by the Clan MacLaren Society in 1987 to commemorate their 25th anniversary. The plaque proclaims that this place is the ancient rallying point of their clan.

4 A seat below the cairn is a grand place to rest after the climb up here. Sit for a while and enjoy the magnificent views over the meandering line of the River Balvag and the length of Loch Voil with the Braes of Balquhidder rising steeply above it. You can see the route that Rob Roy's funeral procession would have taken from Inverlochlarig down to the village itself, and the churchyard where his body lies. From here, retrace your steps back

down the hill but before reaching the top of the stone steps on which you came up, take the path to the left signposted 'Forest Walk'. This continues downhill following waymarked poles, down some steps and across a small bridge. The path goes through some bracken, over a small stream and then across a stile. Eventually it will pass through a small wood of young native trees before emerging on to the forest road.

5 Turn left here and retrace your steps back downhill over the stile and then turn left to return to reach the car park at the start of the walk. From here enter the churchyard and turn left. Rob Roy's grave is on the left in front of the ruins of a pre-Reformation church.

96 Into the Lost Valley

Visit the valley that was the scene of an infamous massacre

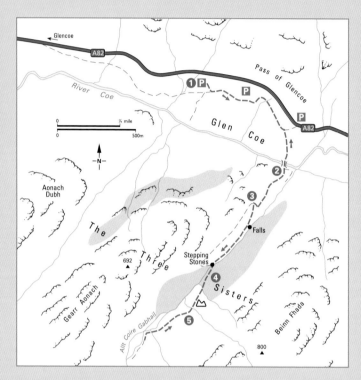

Distance 2.75 miles (4.4km)

Minimum Time 2hrs 15min

Ascent/Gradient 1,050ft (320m) ▲▲▲

Level of Difficulty ●●●

Paths Rugged and stony, stream to wade through

Landscape Crags and mountains

Suggested Map OS Explorer 384 Glen Coe & Glen Etive

Start/Finish Grid reference: NN 168569

Dog Friendliness Dogs must be reasonably fit and agile

Parking Lower of two roadside parking places opposite Gearr Aonach (middle one of Three Sisters)

Public Toilets Glencoe village

1 From the uphill corner of the car park, a faint path slants down to the old road, which is now a well-used wide path. Head up the valley for about 650yds (594m). With the old road continuing as a green track ahead, your path now bends down to the right. It has been rebuilt, with the bog problem solved by scraping down to the bedrock. The path reaches the gorge where the River Coe runs in a geological dyke of softer rock. Descend here on a steep wooden step ladder, to cross a spectacular footbridge.

2 The ascent out of the gorge is on a bare rock staircase. Above, the path runs through regenerating birch wood, which can be very wet on the legs; sheep and deer have been excluded from the wood with a temporary fence. Emerge from this through a high gate. The path, rebuilt in places, runs uphill for 60yds (55m). Here it bends left;

an inconspicuous alternative path continues uphill, which can be used to bypass the narrow path of the main route.

3 The main route contours into the gorge of the Allt Coire Gabhail. It is narrow, with steep drops below. Where there is an alternative of rock slabs and a narrow path just below, the slabs are more secure. You will hear waterfalls, then two fine ones come into view ahead. After passing these, continue between boulders to where the main path bends left to cross the stream below a boulder the size of a small house. (A small path runs on up to right of the stream, but leads nowhere useful.) The river here is wide and fairly shallow. Five or six stepping stones usually allow dry crossing. If the water is above the stones, then it's safer to wade alongside them; however, if the water is more than knee-deep then you should not attempt to make the crossing.

4 A well-built path continues uphill, now with the stream on its right. After 100yds (91m) a lump of rock blocks the way. The path follows a slanting ramp up its right-hand side. It continues uphill, still rebuilt in places, passing above the boulder pile that blocks the valley, the result of two large rockfalls from under Gearr Aonach opposite. At the top of the rockpile the path levels, giving a good view into the Lost Valley.

5 Drop gently to the valley's gravel floor. The stream vanishes into the gravel, to reappear below the boulder pile on the other side. Note where the path arrives at the gravel, as it becomes invisible at that point. Wander up the valley to where the stream vanishes, 0.25 mile (400m) ahead. Anywhere beyond this point is more serious hillwalking than you have done up to now on this walk. Return to the path and follow it back to the start of the walk.

97 The Mysterious Stones of Aberlemno

Inspect Pictish stones and climb to an Iron Age hill-fort

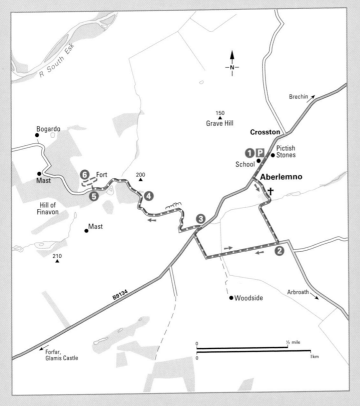

Distance 5 miles (8km)

Minimum Time 1hr 45min

Ascent/Gradient 394ft (120m) ▲▲▲

Level of Difficulty ●●●

Paths Mainly quiet roads but one extremely overgrown area

Landscape Quiet agricultural land and ancient carved stones

Suggested Map OS Explorer 389 Forfar, Brechin & Edzell

Start/Finish Grid reference: TQ 522558

Dog friendliness Overgrown area makes this unsuitable for dogs

Parking Car park by school in Aberlemno

Public Toilets None en route; nearest in Forfar

1 From the car park opposite the Pictish stones turn right along the road, then go first left, signed 'Aberlemno Church and Stone'. Walk past the church – another Pictish stone is found in the churchyard – and follow the road as it bends round to the right and then to the left. Continue until you reach a T-junction.

2 Turn right and follow this road, passing the entrance to Woodside on the left. At the corner, follow the road right. Walk down to join the B9134, turn right and follow this a short distance until you reach a turning on the left.

3 Turn left along this road, signed 'Finavon Hill'. The road winds uphill, past several outcrops, then under a line of pylons. Continue on this road as it skirts a hill.

4 Continue following the road uphill, passing a small loch half-hidden in woodland to the left. Pass an old stone wall on your right, then just beyond a rusty gate in the corner of a field, hop over a section of collapsed wall, taking care to avoid the strand of wire.

5 Head uphill now to explore the turf-covered ramparts of Finavon vitrified fort. Dating from the Iron Age (1000 BC), the hilltop stronghold had walls built of stones that were fused together by tremendous heat. As you walk around the summit, keep a sharp eye out for vitrified material found in the bank.

6 From the hilltop, return to the road and turn left to retrace your steps back to the start of the walk in Aberlemno.

98 The Pass of Ryvoan and the Thieves' Road

Follow a scenic tour in drovers' footsteps near Glenmore village

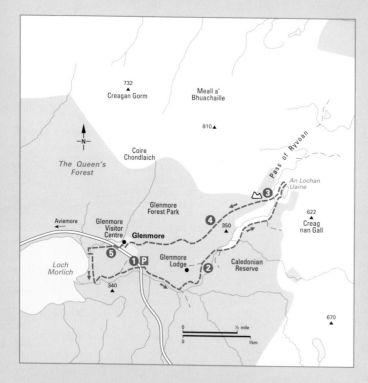

Distance 5 miles (8km)

Minimum Time 2hrs 15min

Ascent/Gradient 400ft (122m) ▲ ▲ ▲

Level of Difficulty ● ● ●

Paths Smooth tracks, one steep ascent, no stile

Landscape Views over Rothiemurchus Forest to Cairngorm

Suggested Map OS Explorer 403 Cairn Gorm & Aviemor

Start/Finish Grid reference: NH 980095

Dog Friendliness Off lead but under close control

Parking Bridge just south of Glenmore village

Public Toilets Glenmore village

1 Head upstream on a sandy track to the left of the river. Interpretation signs explain the flowers of the forest you may come across, many of which are ferns and mosses. After 550yds (503m), turn left on a wide smooth path with blue/yellow waymarkers. Ahead is a gate into Glenmore Lodge rifle range; here the path bends right, to a wide gravel track.

2 Turn right, away from Glenmore Lodge, to cross a concrete bridge into the Caledonian Reserve. Immediately keep ahead on a smaller track (marked by a blue waymarker) as the main one bends right. The track narrows as it heads into the Pass of Ryvoan between steep wooded slopes of pine, birch and scree. At this, the most scenic part of the route, a path turns left, with a blue waymarker, which you take in a moment. Just beyond this, steps on the right lead down to Lochan Uaine. Walk round to the left of the

water on the beach. At the head of the loch a small path leads back up to the track. Turn sharp left, back to the junction already visited; now turn off to the right on to the narrower path with the blue waymarker.

3 This small path crosses some duckboard and heads back down the valley. Very soon it starts to climb steeply to the right, up rough stone steps. When it levels off, the going is easier, although it's still narrow with tree roots. The path reaches a forest road at a bench and a waymarker.

4 Continue to the left along the track. After a clear-felled area with views, the track re-enters trees and slopes downhill into Glenmore village. When you reach the point just above the main road, turn right through a green barrier to reach Glenmore Visitor Centre. Pass through its car park to the main road.

5 Cross to Glenmore shop. Behind a post-box, steps lead down to the campsite. Pass along its right-hand edge to a path into woods. Head left across a footbridge to the shore of Loch Morlich and follow the beaches until another river blocks the way. Turn left along the river bank. Ignore a footbridge, but continue on the wide path with the river on your right. Where the path divides, the smaller branch continues beside the river through bushes to the car park.

Extending the Walk

In good weather you can continue through the Pass of Ryvoan. Return to Glenmore by taking a hill path from the bothy, over the summit of Meall a' Bhuachaille and then down through the Coire Chondlaich.

99 Around the Elegant 'Old Town' of Aberdeen

Explore the sights of old Aberdeen

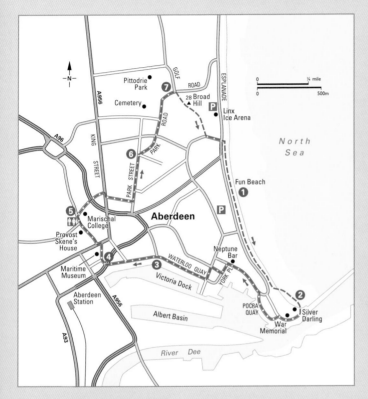

Distance 3.75 miles (6km)

Minimum Time 2hrs

Ascent/Gradient Negligible ▲▲▲

Level of Difficulty ●●●

Paths Mainly pavements; along beach (underwater at high tide)

Landscape Old fishing port

Suggested Map OS Explorer 406 Aberdeen & Banchory

Start/Finish Grid reference: NJ 954067

Dog Friendliness Keep on lead

Parking Esplanade at Fun Beach or Linx Ice Arena

Public Toilets Upperkirkgate, opposite Marischal College

1 From your parking place, head southwards on the promenade, walking beside the shore with the sea on your left. Go down the slipway on to the beach for a short distance to wooden steps on the right and leave the beach to enter a children's play area. (But if the tide is high at the slipway clamber over the sea wall on your right, and pass along a row of fishermen's cottages.)

2 Walk past the Silver Darling restaurant and on into the harbour area. Continue past the war memorial, making sure you keep the blue storage tanks to your left, and go along Pocra Quay as it bends to the right. Turn left into York Street and then when you reach the Neptune bar turn left into York Place. Take the first right, the first left and the second right to emerge on Waterloo Quay.

3 Where Waterloo Quay becomes Commerce Street, turn left into Regent Quay and then at the T-junction cross the dual carriageway at pedestrian lights. Turn left and then first right to reach Aberdeen Maritime Museum and John Ross's House. (Ross was Lord Provost of Aberdeen in 1710–11.) If you have time, visit the Maritime Museum.

4 From here head along Exchequer Row, to turn left into Union Street. At once turn right into Broad Street, where you will find Provost Skene's House on the left, reached by passing underneath an office block.

5 Continue ahead past Marischal College (which houses the Marischal Museum), turn right into Littlejohn Street, and then cross North Street. At the end of Meal Market Street,

turn right into King Street and then left into Frederick Street. At the junction with Park Street turn left and keep walking ahead until the road crosses a railway.

6 Shortly after the crossing is a roundabout. Head slightly right along Park Road. Follow the road through the Trinity Cemetery and towards Pittodrie Park, which is the home of Aberdeen Football Club, to the junction with Golf Road.

7 At the junction with Golf Road, turn up right, on the well-made path over Broad Hill. There are wide views of the sea and Aberdeen. At the path end, turn left to a roundabout with subtropical plants on the Esplanade. The shoreline promenade leads back to your car.

100 Loch an Eilein's Castle and Ord Ban

Take a tour through ancient pines around a picturesque loch

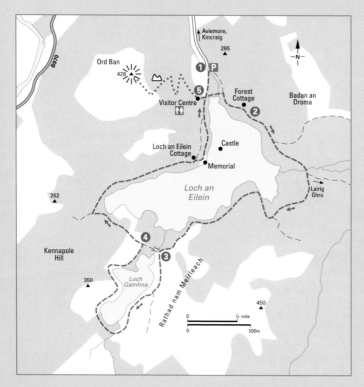

Distance 4.25 miles (6.8km)

Minimum Time 1hr 45min

Ascent/Gradient 100ft (30m) ▲▲▲

Level of Difficulty ●●●

Paths Wide smooth paths, optional steep hill with high ladder stile

Landscape Ancient pine forest around loch

Suggested Map OS Explorer 403 Cairn Gorm & Aviemore

Start/Finish Grid reference: NH 897084

Dog Friendliness Keep on lead on Rothiemurchus Estate

Parking Estate car park near Loch an Eilein, charges apply

Public Toilets Visitor centre

1 From the end of the car park at the beginning of the walk, a made-up path leads to the visitor centre. Turn left to cross the end of Loch an Eilein, then turn right on a smooth, sandy track. The loch shore is near by on the right; there are paths leading down to it if you wish to visit. Just past a red-roofed house, a deer fence runs across, with a gate.

2 The track now becomes a wide, smooth path, which runs close to the loch side. After a bridge, the main track forks right to pass a bench backed by a flat boulder. The smaller path on the left leads high into the hills and through the famous pass of the Lairig Ghru, eventually to Braemar. After crossing a stream at a low concrete footbridge, the path bends right for 120yds (110m) to a junction. Just beyond the junction you'll find a footbridge with wooden handrails.

3 To shorten the walk, cross this footbridge and go along the main track, passing Point 4 in 170yds (155m). For a longer walk, turn left before the footbridge on to a narrower path that will pass around Loch Gamhna. This loch soon appears on your right-hand side. Where the path forks, keep right to pass along the loch side, across its head (rather boggy) and back along its far side, to rejoin the wider path around Loch an Eilein. Turn left here.

4 Continue around Loch an Eilein, with the water on your right, to a reedy corner of the loch. About 55yds (50m) further, the path turns right, signposted 'footpath'. After a gate, turn right to the loch side and a memorial to Major General Brook Rice who drowned here while skating. Follow the shore until opposite the castle, then go back to the track above. A deer fence (left) leads to the visitor centre.

5 From here, a stiff climb (500ft/152m) can be made on to the rocky little hill of Ord Ban, a superb viewpoint. Cross a ladder stile immediately to the right of the toilet block and follow the deer fence to the right for 150yds (137m), to a point behind the car park. Just behind one of the lowest birches on the slope, a small indistinct path zig-zags up the slope. It slants to the left to avoid crags, then crosses a small rock slab (take care if wet) and continues on to the summit. Descend by the same path.

101 Seeing Sea Eagles at Portree Bay

Celebrate the success of a determined conservation effort

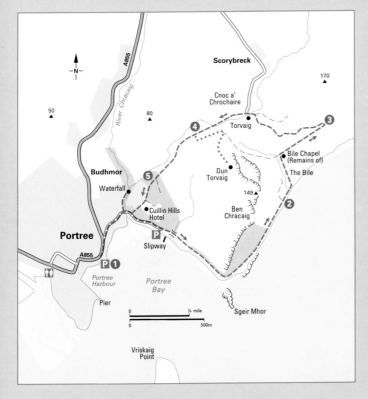

Distance 3.5 miles (5.7km)

Minimum Time 1hr 15min

Ascent/Gradient 459ft (140m) ▲▲▲

Level of Difficulty ●●●

Paths Smooth, well-made paths, farm track, 3 stiles

Landscape Views across Minch from wooded coast and hill above

Suggested Map OS Explorer 409 Raasay, Rona & Scalpay or 410 Skye – Portree & Bracadale

Start Grid reference: NG 485436

Dog Friendliness Dogs on leads through farmland, scoop poop on shore path

Parking On A855 (Staffin Road) above Portree Bay. Another small parking area near slipway

Public Toilets Town centre, just off main square

1 Turn off the main A855 on to a lane signed 'Budh Mor', to walk down to the shoreline and then continue to a small parking area. A tarred path continues along the shore past a slipway. After a footbridge, it passes under hazels that show the typical ground-branching habit of bushes formerly coppiced, cut back every seven years for firewood. The path passes below a viewpoint with flagpoles and then rounds the headland to reach the edge of a level green field called The Bile.

2 A wall runs up the edge of The Bile. A sign points up left for 'Scorybreck'; ignore it and go through a small gate ahead. A path leads into the corner of The Bile field. Go up its left edge and across the top, to a stile. Cross the top of the next field on an old path to a stile at its corner. You will see a track beyond.

3 Turn sharp left, up the track. At the top it passes through two gates to reach a stony road just to the right of Torvaig. Turn left past the house and cross the foot of a tarred road into a gently descending track. It runs down between two large corrugated sheds and then through to a gate with a stile.

4 The grassy path ahead leads down into Portree, but you can take a short, rather rough, diversion to Dun Torvaig (an ancient fortified hilltop) above. For the dun, turn left along the fence, and left again on a well-made path above. It leads to a kissing gate above the two sheds. Turn sharp right along the fence for a few steps, then bear left around the base of a small outcrop and head straight up on a tiny path to the dun. Remnants of dry-stone walling can be seen around the summit. Return to the

well-made path, passing above Point 4 to join the wall on the right. The path leads down under goat willows into a wood where it splits; stay close to the wall.

5 At the first houses (The Parks Bungalow 5), keep downhill on a tarred street. On the left is the entrance to the Cuillin Hills Hotel. A few steps later, fork right on to a stony path. At the shore road, turn right across a stream and right again on a path that runs up for 60yds (55m) to a craggy little waterfall. Return to the shore road and turn right to the walk start.

102 Strathpeffer and the Rogie Falls

Look for a leaping salmon at a wild forest waterfall

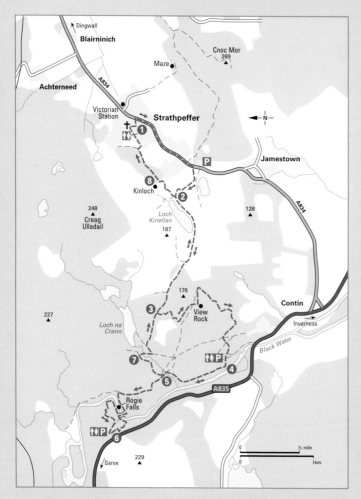

Distance 10 miles (16.1km)

Minimum Time 5hrs

Ascent/Gradient 1,200ft (366m) ▲▲▲

Level of Difficulty ●●●

Paths Waymarked paths and tracks, no stiles

Landscape Plantation, wild forest and riverside

Suggested Map OS Explorer 437 Ben Wyvis & Strathpeffer

Start/Finish Grid reference: NH 483582

Dog Friendliness Keep on lead for section past Loch Kinellan

Parking Main square, Strathpeffer

Public Toilets At start, Contin (Point 4) and Rogie Falls car parks

1 Go along the main road to Contin. At the edge of town, turn right signed 'Garve' then, at a bend, turn left at another signpost.

2 Follow a track left of Loch Kinellan. As it bends right, go up to a plantation, then into forest for 0.5 mile (800m) to a signpost.

3 Turn left for View Rock on a good path with green waymarkers. At View Rock, a side-path diverts to the right for the viewpoint, then rejoins. After a long descent, follow green waymarkers downhill. At a forest road go straight over, and across two further forest roads to Contin Forest car park.

4 At the end of the car park, pick up a wide path. Where red waymarkers turn right, follow deer-head markers to a forest road. Turn left and in 80yds (73m) bear left, downhill.

5 After 600yds (549m) take a track left signed 'Rogie Falls Bridge'. Cross a footbridge below the falls and turn right; after 0.25 mile (400m) bend left. Cross rocky ground to a junction. Turn right, to Rogie Falls car park.

6 Leave through a wooden arch and follow green waymarkers to the bridge. Retrace the outward route to Point 5 and turn left up a forest road to where a fainter track crosses.

7 Turn right down the smaller track to a signpost, then left, signed 'Strathpeffer'. After 600yds (549m), at the signpost of Point 3, go ahead and retrace the outward route to Point 2. Turn left. At Kinloch house go right, then left through kissing gates into a plantation with a signpost for Strathpeffer.

8 Follow the main path until you see Strathpeffer. At the next junction bear right then right into town. Go left past a church with a square steeple, then right to the main square.

103 Looking Into Scotland's Great Wilderness

Take a gentle ramble while gazing with wonder far into the wilds

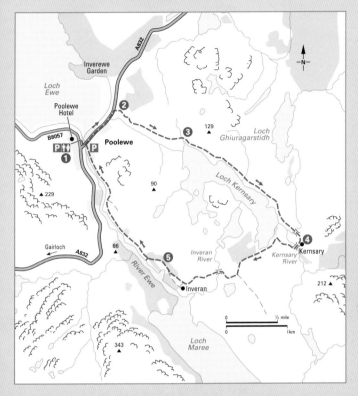

Distance 6.5 miles (10.4km)

Minimum Time 2hrs 45min

Ascent/Gradient 250ft (76m) ▲▲▲

Level of Difficulty ●●●

Paths Mostly good, but one short rough, wet section, 3 stiles

Landscape Moorland and loch side

Suggested Map OS Explorer 434 Gairloch & Loch Ewe

Start/Finish Grid reference: NG 857808

Dog Friendliness Close control on moorland and tracks carrying estate traffic

Parking In Poolewe, just up B8057 side street

Public Toilets At start

1 A kissing gate beside the public toilets leads to a path that crosses the Marie Curie Field of Hope to the main road. Turn left to cross the bridge over the River Ewe and then head all the way through the village. At the 40mph derestriction sign, there's a white cottage on the right. Beside it, a tarred trackway has a Scottish Rights of Way Society signpost for Kernsary.

2 Follow the track over a cattle grid as far as a new track that forks off to the left. After 50yds (46m), keep ahead on a path with a wall on its left. It passes through a kissing gate into Cnoc na Lise, the Garden Hill. This has been replanted as a community wood with oak and birch trees. Another kissing gate leads out of the young wood. The good, reconstructed path runs through gorse and then under a

low-voltage power line. It crosses a low spur to a fine view of Loch Kernsary and the remote, steep-sided hills of the Great Wilderness, then goes over a stream to the loch side.

3 The path follows the left-hand shore of the loch, passing through patches of birch scrub. After a stile, near the loch head, it suddenly deteriorates, becoming a braided trod of boulder and bog. Once past the loch head, slant to the left down a meadow to find a footbridge beneath the branches of an oak tree. Head up, with a fence on your right, to join a track beside Kernsary farm.

4 Turn right, through a gate. Follow the track past the farm, to a culvert crossing of the Kernsary River. This becomes a ford only after heavy rain. If needed, you will find a footbridge

70yds (64m) upstream. After crossing, turn right on a smooth track. The new track bears left, away from Loch Kernsary towards the hollow containing Loch Maree. After the bridge over the Inveran River is a gate with a ladder stile. Signs welcoming responsible walkers and cyclists reflect the principles of the Letterewe Accord. Soon come the first views of Loch Maree. The driveway of Inveran house joins from the left and the track becomes tarred.

5 At a sign, 'Blind Corners', a green track on the left leads down to the point where the narrow loch imperceptibly becomes a wide river. Return to the main track and follow it above and then beside the River Ewe. It reaches Poolewe just beside the bridge.

Acknowledgements

Walks written and compiled by:
Chris Bagshaw, Kate Barrett, Bill Birkett, Sheila Bowker, Nick Channer, Paddy Dillon, Rebecca Ford, David Foster, John Gillham, David Hancock, Des Hannigan, Tom Hutton, Tom Kelly, Dennis Kelsall, Deborah King, Andrew McCloy, Moira McCrossan, Terry Marsh, John Morrison, Andrew Noyce, Nick Reynolds, Beau Riffenburgh and Liz Cruwys, Julie Royle, Jon Sparks, Ann F Stonehouse, Hugh Taylor, Ronald Turnbull, Sue Viccars, David Winpenny.

The Automobile Association would like to thank the following photographers, companies and picture libraries for their assistance in the preparation of this book. Abbreviations for the picture credits are as follows – (t) top; (b) bottom; (c) centre; (l) left; (r) right; (AA) AA World Travel Library.

9 AA/M Kipling; 10 AA/J Wood; 12 AA/T Mackie; 15 AA/A Lawson; 16 AA/J A Tims; 126 AA/M Kipling

Every effort has been made to trace the copyright holders, and we apologise in advance for any accidental errors. We would be happy to apply any corrections in the following edition of this publication.

Previous page
The distinctive hill
of Roseberry Topping,
North York Moors